"Hollander's clear, brisk style packs every paragraph with provocative ideas. What is the T-shirt but male underwear with an imprinted motto, a provisional tattoo?" —Robert Taylor, *The Boston Globe*

"Hollander rides her theories like a surfer, and her wittiest prose retains the note of generosity that gives human curiosity its moral weight." —Diane Middlebrook, *The Los Angeles Times*

"To fully appreciate the suit's enduring aesthetic and erotic success, Hollander treats us to an unfailingly insightful, creative, and provocative history of modern fashion. She maintains a rich cultural context while pondering the interplay between sex and the imagination, idealized gender roles and clothing, fashion's unreliability and irony, and the crucial roles the printing press and the camera have played in Western fashion's global dominance." —*Booklist*

"Imagine Pauline Kael swooning at the rack of gray men's suits at Brooks Brothers." —Richard Rodriguez, *Newsday*

"Iconoclastic, continually stimulating." —*Publishers Weekly*

"Hollander, with great cheerfulness and delicacy of perception, embraces the chaos in individual determinations in any art." —John Updike, *The New Yorker*

SEX
AND
SUITS

ALSO BY ANNE HOLLANDER

Seeing Through Clothes
Moving Pictures

SEX
AND
SUITS

ANNE
HOLLANDER

KODANSHA INTERNATIONAL
New York • Tokyo • London

TO THE MEMORY OF MY MOTHER,
JEAN BASSETT LOESSER

KODANSHA AMERICA, INC.

114 FIFTH AVENUE, NEW YORK, NEW YORK 10011, U.S.A.

KODANSHA INTERNATIONAL LTD.

17-14 OTOWA 1-CHOME, BUNKYO-KU, TOKYO 112, JAPAN

PUBLISHED IN 1995 BY KODANSHA AMERICA, INC.

BY ARRANGEMENT WITH ALFRED A. KNOPF, INC.

FIRST PUBLISHED IN 1994 BY ALFRED A. KNOPF, INC.

THIS IS A KODANSHA GLOBE BOOK.

LIBRARY OF CONGRESS CATALOGING-IN-PUBLICATION DATA

Hollander, Anne.
Sex and suits : the evolution of modern dress / Anne Hollander.
p.   cm. — (Kodansha globe)
Originally published: New York : Knopf, 1994.
Includes bibliographical references (p.   ) and index.
ISBN 1-56836-101-7
1. Costume—Social aspects.   2. Men's clothing—History.
3. Costume—History.   I. Title.   II. Series.
GT525.H65   1995
391'.1—dc20   95-34403

BOOK DESIGN BY IRIS WEINSTEIN

PRINTED IN THE UNITED STATES OF AMERICA

95 96 97 98 99   Q/FF   10 9 8 7 6 5 4 3 2 1

CONTENTS

ILLUSTRATIONS

SEX
AND
SUITS

I. INTRODUCTION

SEX AND MODERN FORM

ALTHOUGH MALE heads of state wear suits at summit meetings, male job applicants wear them to interviews, and men accused of rape and murder wear them in court to help their chances of acquittal, the pants-jacket-shirt-and-tie costume, formal or informal, is often called boring or worse. Like other excellent and simple things we cannot do without, men's suits have lately acquired an irksome esthetic flavor, I would say an irritating *perfection*. Their integrated, subtle beauty is often an affront to post-modern sensibilities, to eyes and minds attuned to the jagged and turbulent climate of the late twentieth century. Current millennial impulses tend toward disintegration, in style as in politics; but men's suits are neither post-modern nor minimalist, multicultural nor confessional—they are relentlessly modern, in the best classic sense. They seem moreover to be surviving, despite their current bad press and an undeniable dip in the number being sold during difficult economic times.

The following reflections come from considering modern men's tailored clothes. By this I mean suits, in particular; but I more generally mean the whole range of tailored jackets, trousers, waistcoats, overcoats, shirts and neckties that make up standard masculine civil costume all over the world. Why has this sartorial scheme lasted such a long time?

3

What accounts for its stylistic force and endurance? What does male tailoring have to do with modern sexuality, male and female? How does it relate to fashion, present and past? How does it relate to modern design, of clothes or anything else? Why have women wanted so desperately to copy it ever since it was invented? And what is its future?

Everyone knows that clothes are social phenomena; changes in dress *are* social changes. It is further said that political and social changes are mirrored in dress; but since suits have stayed virtually the same for two hundred years, their continuity must illustrate something else. I believe the staying power of male tailoring shows how visual form can have its own authority, its own self-perpetuating symbolic and emotional force. This is a modern belief; and the very way modern suits look expresses the thought. It is expounded by their intrinsically abstract formal character, together with their abiding evolutionary character—their look of looking like themselves, even while their style keeps slightly changing. Their message of purely formal continuity, even with all the fragmentation many examples are now undergoing, apparently still carries deep satisfaction in the contemporary world.

By staying the same while undergoing constant internal changes, male tailoring acquired more virtue and new value throughout its life, instead of losing force or currency. It has gathered power rather than dissipating its force during its two centuries of fluctuation, so that its satisfactions have been cumulative. By not vanishing, but instead shifting ground and visual emphasis, and also shifting their social and sexual meaning, tailored suits have proved themselves infinitely dynamic, possessed of their own fashionable energy. Rebellion against such insistent strength is only natural, especially in the present historical climate; but notably it is the wearing of suits that is now simply being avoided, not the design of them that is being corrupted or abandoned. In the realm of design itself, their power is being provisionally sidestepped, not attacked; and a direct attack I believe would lose. One reason is that women are obviously not finished with the motifs of male tailoring, even if some men are presently restless in them. More is coming, in line with what is already here, which is already extremely various.

Far from abolishing well-tailored suits along with other old modes left over from the craft tradition, advances in technology and economic organization during the past two centuries have in fact been bent on *pre-*

serving the character of men's tailoring and spreading its availability, making it ever more flexible. Preserving the good looks of men's suits has not been a deliberately conservationist, antiquarian effort; it has happened by itself, in response to some huge collective fantasy that is obviously still potent.

I would say this is the fantasy of modern form as the proper material vessel of both beauty and power, of positive sexuality. To convey all these things at once, modern rules of material design suggest that all lines, shapes and volumes, whatever their arrangement, should produce a visual model of dynamic coherence and integrity, rather than a model of complex display, or one of crude force, or one of the latter overlaid by the former. For really effective impact, all ornament should form part of the total composition, and all materials be candidly undisguised.

In this century, as old fashion plates show, the abstract shapes and plain textures of modern suits were linked to the visual vocabulary of modern abstract art; but even more tellingly and more consistently, they shared in the formal authority of modern practical design. One important thing it and they both continue to have is erotic appeal, in the confidently forceful mode. Suits are still sexy, just like cars and planes. One even deeper secret of their erotic appeal is the unified ease that seems to link them to the unselfconscious natural dress of animals. Panthers and gazelles are often compared to cars, too, in visual advertising; their easy-fitting suits, which give good figures to all examples, offer an ideal for a modern mode of clothing design that seeks to ape the efficiency and elegance of nature. Nature, of course, ordains that human beings be completed by clothing, not left bare in their own insufficient skins.

A LONGING FOR compelling integrity in design seems to have arisen in the West in the second half of the eighteenth century, after the decline of Rococo taste, and in connection with the Enlightenment. The classic male tailoring now so universally familiar was originally Neoclassic. It was invented and perfected between about 1780 and 1820, just when the simplest visual motifs in Classical design were suggesting the force and clarity of Greek democracy and Roman technology. Both of these became erotically as well as politically appealing; basic Greek or Roman seemed the right form in which to cast the various new social and emotional aspirations of the moment.

The same fantasy was recapitulated for art and design in this century, in the modern style invented after the decline of Victorian taste, and in connection with industrial expansion and practical democracy. The modern material version had aims and sources different from the Neoclassical one; but in the realm of male tailoring—though not in architecture, domestic design nor female fashion—the same forms themselves served uninterruptedly down to our own time, despite late Romantic, Victorian, and Art Nouveau contributions and interventions.

Suits kept their male sexual thrill, which apparently dwelt in the cumulative force of the form itself. Although the tailoring scheme was perpetually being remodelled by fashion, it was never given up nor radically undermined. It was the context and connotations of tailored suits that changed, not their basic form. Rhetoric about them has periodically added new meaning to them, a great deal of it unfavorable even at periods other than ours, while they have nevertheless persisted in staying the same and staying around.

I HAVE USED modern men's tailoring as the foundation of my story because I have come to believe that male dress was always essentially more advanced than female throughout fashion history, and tended to lead the way, to set the standard, to make the esthetic propositions to which female fashion responded. Men's clothes since the Middle Ages have been more formally interesting and innovative and less conservative than women's; and I find that the invention of modern suits is a good example of the same trend. But I also believe that any true account of clothing must consider both sexes together, so I will continue to do that in all the rest of these speculations.

In modern fashion, the sexuality of clothing is its first quality; clothes address the personal self first of all, and only afterwards the world. Little children learn that clothes give them private identity, defining inward ideas of the personal body which begin with ideas of its sexuality. In the continuing process of such definition, public adult dress eventually becomes a reciprocal sexual gesture in a generally two-sexed world. The present popular excitement about transvestism only shows how deeply we still believe in symbolically separating the clothes of men and women, even though they dress the same on many occasions.

. . .

BUT NO MATTER how similar the clothes of men and women may appear, or how different, the arrangements of each are always being made with respect to the other. Male and female clothing, taken together, illustrates what people wish the relation between men and women to be, besides indicating the separate peace each sex is making with fashion or custom at any given time. Without looking at what men are wearing, it's impossible to understand women's clothes, and vice versa. The history of dress, including its current history, so far has to be perceived as a duet for men and women performing on the same stage. There may come a time when sexuality is not visualized in clothing as rightly divided into two main categories; but so far it still is.

AT THE NEO-CLASSIC moment, tailored suits put a final seal of disapproval on gaudy clothes for serious men, whatever their class. At the same time, they confirmed and approved a sharpened visual separation between the dress of men and women, whatever their class. The strong, simple forms of modern design, as they were first conceived for Neo-classic architecture, were perceived as naturally masculine. Esthetic theory at the time is full of words like "virile" and "muscular" to describe the proper character of buildings created with the new simplicity of form based on ancient prototypes. An analogue in dress would thus naturally occur in male civil costume, and not in feminine fashion. Women were long since understood to follow old habits of adornment, once common to both sexes, that were still considered their abiding privilege, perhaps even their duty; and women's adherence to variegated display is one thing that has made their clothing essentially more *conservative* than men's. At the Neo-classic moment it was men, not women, who enterprisingly made a radical modern leap in fashion.

That period coincided with the beginning of the Romantic movement, when an acute tension between the sexes was itself an imaginative necessity; and the differing fashions for clothes of the two sexes illustrate this idea very clearly. From that short epoch (with a preparatory run-up during the generation before) dates the custom of putting only women into colorful ornamented fancies and dressing men in simple, dull-finished, undecorated shapes. Fashion thereafter, the fashion of the modern world, would move along a distinctly divided track for the first time in the hundreds of years of its history, taking two separate paths that are only just beginning to converge now. Then, the distinction between male and female clothes became a more volatile matter than it had ever been. It created the most marked feature of the whole modern period until the present disintegrative epoch.

Comparing the history of dress before about 1800 with what came afterwards, you can see what sartorial modernity seems to consist of, the qualities that distinguish the clothes of the modern world. Female dress always makes a strong, almost theatrical visual claim, but male tailored costume sets the real standard. The tailored costume I refer to moreover includes its informal versions, the sportswear and country leisure wear that shared the scene with men's formal city wear for work or play. Work-clothes, the jackets of lumbermen and the jeans of cattlemen, were also part of the general scheme, developing at the same time in the early nineteenth century. Male garments for golf and tennis, or for hunting, shooting, sailing or fishing, can be seen to share in it, despite their great differences when viewed from the standpoint of strict social usage. Gradual "modernizations" in female costume since 1800 have mainly consisted of trying to approach the male ideal more closely, using an assortment of its motifs.

This ideal offers a complete envelope for the body that is nevertheless made in separate, layered, detached pieces. Arms, legs and trunk are visibly indicated but not tightly fitted, so that large movements of the trunk or limbs don't put awkward strain on seams or fastenings, and the lumps and bumps of the individual body's surface are harmoniously glossed over, never emphatically modelled. The separate elements of the costume overlap, rather than attaching to each other, so that great physical mobility is possible without creating awkward gaps in the composition. The whole costume may thus settle itself naturally when the body stops moving, so that its own poise is effortlessly resumed after a swift dash or sudden struggle. Meanwhile languid sprawling will cause the costume to disarrange its easy fit into attractively casual folds which form a fluid set of grace-notes for the relaxed body, and which also obligingly resume a smooth shape if the wearer must quickly get up and stand straight.

The costume is thus socially formal and informal at the same time,

8

obedient to the flow of circumstances. Decorative elements are integrated with the overall scheme, so that nothing sticks out, slides off, twists around, gets bruised, goes limp or catches on anything. All this combines an invincible harmony of independent design with ease of use and a true echo of underlying bodily shape and action. It is universally flattering, because it does not insist on specific bodily detail. It reflects the modern esthetic principles that were conceived out of Neo-classic aspirations in the late eighteenth century, just like modern democratic impulses. Also like them (as embodied in the United States Constitution, for example), it proposes an ideal of self-perpetuating order, flexible and almost infinitely variable.

By contrast, women's fashion after 1800 consistently suggested quite different ideas, none of them modern at all, most of them following quite ancient and general sartorial custom. The effect of deliberate display sets the tone, supported by the effect of deliberate trouble taken for the purpose—elaborate headwear, difficult footwear, cosmetics, extraneous adornments and accessories, constriction and extension. I would emphasize that this scheme embodies the prescribed character of elegance *for both sexes* in past epochs all over the world, in both modish and traditional folk styles of costume everywhere, and for self-respecting persons in most layers of society.

Nineteenth- and twentieth-century women's clothes simply kept it up. They continued to demonstrate the primal and often sacred original purpose of dress, which is to represent, in terms of self-imposed and noticeable bodily applications—which may include distortion and disfigurement—the spiritual aspirations, the imaginative projections, and the practical sacrifices that divide self-aware human adults from careless infants and innocent beasts. This is a great and deep idea, but it is not modern.

There was nothing modern about modern women's clothes until the female imitation of the modern male scheme was gradually accomplished during the course of this century. Emancipated women seeking to modernize their clothes found no better way than to imitate what men had done a century earlier, copying the idea of a loosely fitting envelope that would reveal its own clear tailored shape while suggesting that of the body under it, and allow concerted movement of invented dress and living body together. Women's clothes of the 1920's and 1930's actually achieved the modern ideal; but they kept to the distinctively feminine scheme, and the sexes kept their traditional separation. The ancient universal belief in taking visible trouble to dress up prevailed continuously in modern women's fashion, promoting the curiosities and varieties which essentially make a very old story. This meant that men had nothing fundamentally new and interesting to learn from women's clothes throughout the period; their modernization was already complete. They had long since gone beyond cosmetics, carefully curled hair, problematic shoes, and elaborate decoration. Fashion for men instead took the form of continuing to modify the Neo-classic tailored conception, with some interesting advances that were usually inspired (as the original scheme also was) by male active sports gear, work-clothes and military and naval dress. Male costume, committed to the modern look of effortlessly integrated formal design, tended to hide any discomfort and trouble it might actually produce for the wearer.

WHAT FASHION IS

PARTLY IN RESPONSE to the great gulf dividing the sexes during these last two modern centuries, the definition of fashion has undergone a sharp and limiting reduction. With the arrival of collective certainty that powerful men must dress soberly and similarly, and that women's clothes must carry all the burden of deliberate personal fantasy, fashion in dress became "Fashion," one of the huge new industries aimed specifically at female consumers, instead of being something in which men or women might properly show the same kind of interest.

At the end of the twentieth century, "Fashion" still chiefly means the currency of variation in women's clothes, perceived while it is being invented and marketed exactly as variations in the entertainment business are perceived, and sometimes in connection with them. "Fashion" is what appears by that name in the media and in designers' collections in shops, after first appearing on runways; and just as in all of show business, it is now connected with famous names and their famous characteristic associations. The stars of "Fashion" arrive, thrive and fade, new postures and themes flourish until dimmed or swamped by others, all in the context of vast and thrilling corporate risk. Actual women take "Fashion" seriously or not, depending on their lives, means and views; but they may all believe that it is something legitimately possible for them, something any woman may ignore if she likes but always has an absolute right to take part in.

Men's clothes clearly do not participate directly in "Fashion," since "Men's Fashion" is an acknowledged subset, and has scarcely any of the fame and resonance attaching to "Fashion." Some effort is now being made to even the score and make something more publicly exciting out of "Men's Fashion," but it has a long way to go. Most men, in accordance with modern rules, are still quite comfortable ignoring "Men's Fashion" in its show-businesslike aspects, and feeling that it is not actually available to them nor even really aimed at them. The general idea is that only a few care, and they are not important. Very remarkable and fantastic male modes of dressing, on the other hand, are continually adopted chiefly by the powerless, those not in the main stream of action. Their importance in mainstream fashion for all men, however, is growing, along with a current dissatisfaction with traditional male modernity.

Meanwhile everybody has to get dressed in the morning and go about the day's business. What everybody wears to do this has taken different forms in the West for about seven hundred years, and that is what fashion is, now or ever, and what I always mean by the term, minus quotes. Fashion has affected both sexes equally, and nobody with eyes escapes it; it is now the general modern condition of all Western clothing, and it has increasingly become so since the Early Modern period. It now appears in multiple manifestations, so that many different fashions, small and large, are flourishing at the same time. Most fashion in dress is adopted with the conscious wish not to look fashionable, but to look right. "Fashionable" is merely one very consciously achieved way of looking fashionable—that is, right—at any given time or place.

The shifty character of what looks right is not new, and was never a thing deliberately created to impose male will on females, or capitalist will on the population, or designers' will on public taste. Long before the days of industrialized fashion, stylistic motion in Western dress was enjoying a profound emotional importance, giving a dynamically poetic visual cast to people's lives, and making Western fashion hugely compelling all over the world. With new global consciousness, it now appeals to civilizations that have never had a history of fashionable cycles, and that were proud of not having one. Fashion has its own manifest virtue, not unconnected with the virtues of individual freedom and uncensored imagination that still underlie democratic ideals.

We are now accustomed to the idea that professional designers are the ones who deliberately invent fashion for the garment business to produce, the way movie studios produce the work of screenwriters and directors. Specific credit for the extraordinary phenomena of fashion in the past, however, is quite hard to fix; they were flourishing and changing long before they were attributed to individual creative effort. For six centuries, individual inventors were never held responsible for the remarkable clothing worn by peasants, burghers or nobles—either fashion or custom created the form. Only anecdotes remain about the momentary effects, adopted spontaneously by a royal mistress or a political star, that set a certain fashion for a time. No credit to any imaginative artisan survives, until near the end of the eighteenth century when Rose Bertin became famous for arranging the toilettes of Marie Antoinette. That queen was of course famous for vanity and reckless expenditure, and an accomplice in those vices was a natural accompaniment to her bad reputation.

A close look at what known designers have done in the modern period moreover shows that their work is all remarkably similar at any given time, exactly like the fashionable phenomena of any past period. The collective imagination appears stronger than the individual one, and most designers work to serve it, not their own free inspiration. Innovative genius in modern clothing design has been as rare as any other kind, and the world often only catches up with it later on, when general taste is ready. Meanwhile armies of designers are at work demonstrating that fashion is governing them, just as it does the rest of us, and that they simply aim to please us, if possible, with their specific versions of it. I have therefore continued in the old custom of speaking as if fashion in dress were a force with its own will, something that the collective desire of Western people brought into existence so that it might have an independent life, something designers and public together can only continue to help along its vigorous path.

The rest of this study is about the way fashion functions esthetically and erotically, and used to function so that it eventually produced suits for men, and what happened afterwards in the nineteenth century; about what later happened in this century to both fashion and suits, with respect to new modes of sexual feeling, art, fashion art and design; about how women's clothing became modern, and what effect that has had; and about how clothes of the two sexes are looking, now that the next millennium is about to start. I will continue as always to discuss all clothing as essentially a form of artistic expression, with the same relation to life, the same accountability and unaccountability. In speaking of dress I am always concerned either with line and form or with sex and poetry, not with money and power. I'm working from the idea that sexuality and imagination are what originally produce the extraordinary formal imagery that can cause money and power to be reflected in clothes, along with the other things reflected there.

Clothes show that visual form has its own capacity, independent of practical forces in the world, to satisfy people, perpetuate itself, and make its own truth apart from linguistic reference and topical allusion. Forms survive and are used again and again in many variants, attaching different temporary meaning to their abiding visual appeal. The language of clothes is essentially wordless—that is what it was created to be, so that it can operate freely below the level of conscious thought and utterance. Fashion, like art, shows that visual satisfaction has its own remarkable laws, and that these are related to sexuality in its imaginative vein. The relation between the imagery of fashion and real conditions in society is thus complicated by the imaginative process, which has rich perversities and denials built into it that defy any easy analysis of what is creating fashion's visual schemes. Fashion is therefore constantly complicated by the rhetoric that surrounds it, the emotionally or commercially motivated remarks that can cast a transforming spell on its formal elements. As a consequence, fashions often look no more ridiculous than interpretations of them do.

II. THE WORK OF FASHION

FASHION, NON-FASHION AND ANTI-FASHION

WHAT MAKES FASHION different from other forms of clothing? How do the differences work, and how have they been perceived? The world has invented many ways to dress since the beginning of its history, but fashion has been distinct from them all, arriving in the late Middle Ages to propose a compelling new system for Western elegance. Western fashion has ever since kept its own unique method of dealing with the human body, creating an eventful visual history quite separate from what I call non-fashion, the sum of the other developments in dress and adornment that have been conceived and continued all over the globe. Western feelings about fashion have varied; and so has Western sentiment about non-fashion, which still forms an ever-present counterpoint to fashion in the world of clothed appearance. The characteristics of each are worth examining, to account for some of those feelings.

FASHION IN DRESS is committed to risk, subversion and irregular forward movement. It creates quick shifts of visual design for the whole body, but it also affects tiny details and governs slow changes, so it seems to change its own hidden design, not just the most noticeable shapes of clothes. Essentially unreliable, fashion is also relentlessly secular, at odds with the ceremonial and unifying esthetic impulses that produce garments like the *chador* or the *sari;* and it always takes the ironic view of anything time-honored. Its quotes from old traditions, its own or others, tend to be oblique and inaccurate, outrageous and funny. Fashion visually celebrates the irrational, preserving tension rather than seeking resolution; and it relishes the quick pleasure of provisional arrangements instead of seeking permanent esthetic solutions, or anything purely practical and useful. Even in the relatively calm history of modern male tailoring, fashion has been bumptiously alive, using new cuffless trousers to make cuffs look ridiculous, or bringing on skinny ties to trump wide ones.

Fashion instantly mocks sensible inventions in clothing, subjecting them to unfunctional usage as soon as they appear, so they can seem authentically desirable and never merely convenient. This has happened to belts, pockets, and fastenings of every kind, to helmets, aprons, and boots; they are no sooner put into use than put into play. Convenience is not sacrificed; but it quickly takes second place to the delicious look of convenience. In the imaginative art of fashion, such a look satisfies a much stronger desire than any wish for a useful thing: in actual wear, the look always outlasts the use.

ALL THIS MAKES fashion "modern" by nature, when modern means being consciously concerned with process, both social and personal, and following an ideal of deliberate modification rather than one of preservation, where change occurs only in a gradual drift promoted by chance. But above all fashion is a modern *art,* because its formal changes illustrate this idea of process at a remove, as other modern art has done; it is always a representation. Fashion makes its own sequence of imaginative pictures in its own formal medium, which has its own history; it doesn't simply create a direct visual mirror of cultural facts. Its images have no single or simple relation to external changes and differences. They form a sequential art, an emblematic projection of life, a visual analogue to the sort of common experience that is founded on social facts, but that takes its forms from inward life—common memories and allusions, perverse current references, things carefully learned by rote, other things learned by half-conscious habit, obscure jokes, open secrets, and a host of unconscious, collective fantasies always in flux through time.

Most of the meaningful references in fashion are submerged in the look of ordinary dressed persons at any given moment, because fashion is mainly engaged in acting out its own formal history, and reacts most vividly only to itself, like many other modern arts. What always shows first is the sign of fashion's own life, the shifting flow of shape and line—shoulders thickening and skirts shortening or the opposite, a neatness following a sloppiness or the opposite, former underwear used as outerwear or the opposite, long hair or short hair, beards or no beards, all lingering apparitions incessantly looking changed in the light of a few new ones.

This dance follows fashion's own uneven rhythm, which shifts its elements, large and small, at different rates. For a while, the form of notches in lapels may change quickly but whole jackets remain much the same; then lapels may become very narrow or very wide, or vanish for a time and come back; then whole jackets may change shape, as shoulders expand and waists tighten, while lapels will stay still; then the whole thing will reverse; and finally, much further along in the sequence, jackets themselves may eventually become obsolete, in favor of tunics or whatever. While changes are occurring, a palimpsest of old modes always remains on the scene, to confuse the future historian. Small movements in fashion can be traced; but they seem to have no direct relation to changes in the social fabric, even though they go on at the same time. They show fashion flexing its muscles and doing a little shadow-boxing.

Because of its large emotional foundation, fashion always reflects the temper of history; but it's not really perfect as a mirror except as a temporal index—those collars were worn just at that time, these others started sooner and lasted longer; those were first worn in Rome, and later appeared in Madrid; this sort of trouser first appeared west of the Mississippi, and later joined this other sort on the East Coast. Understanding the element of immediate political importance—these colors were used for three years to show support for a certain cause, this pattern showed protest against another—may help to date a fashion; but the actual relation between the politics and the form the fashion takes always remains somewhat uncertain, since people often wear things for perverse reasons or without reasons. Because of fashion's indirect representational function, assigning an incontrovertible immediate meaning to formal details is almost impossible. The real expressive meaning will by definition escape established expectation and float freely in the imaginative world among unconscious aspirations and nostalgias, many of them irretrievable. Only the form itself can sometimes be traced back to its formal source or sources.

Form in fashion has been shown to move in very general cycles, so that what suddenly looks wonderful may suggest what looked wonderful about twenty-five years earlier, or even fifty or a hundred; and the change therefore is called a revival. But the social meaning is confined simply to who wears it at the moment, not why; and who wears it changes, just as form itself does. The flow of modern culture requires that fashion offer fluid imagery for its own sake, to keep visually present the ideal of perpetual contingency. Meaning is properly detachable from form, so that the revival of forms from earlier days need have nothing to do with any perception of earlier days; a new impulse makes them visually attractive again, and a new meaning is attached to them. A visual reference to the past can, of course, be deliberate and pointedly historical, with the meaning included; but it never needs to be. Fashion abhors fixity, of form or meaning, of knowledge or feeling, of the past itself.

Fashionable dress thus has a built-in contingent character quite lacking to all ethnic and folk dress, and to most clothes of the ancient world. Traditional dress, everything that I call non-fashion, works differently. It creates its visual projections primarily to illustrate the confirmation of established custom, and to embody the desire for stable meaning even if custom changes—it is normative. Form in non-fashion certainly changes, too; all traditional dress has developed, just as customs have, with some elements becoming vestigial while others gain new vitality as the life of the community continues. But even with considerable change in the look of traditional clothing over time, the formal relation of new to old is direct, a straightforward adaptation, never a detached commentary of the new upon the old, or a subversive attempt to undermine it.

That's because the new does not arise out of a tension intrinsic to the formal vocabulary itself, as it does in fashion. New things may come from outside the tradition, perhaps derived from the dress or possessions of arriving slaves or conquerors, traders or neighbors—or perhaps lately of anthropologists and journalists—without changing the basic conception of costume as custom. The words are related, as in "habit" and "habit"; and we know that habits are adaptable within a rule for stability. In non-fashion, new things are assimilated or simply added, just as in traditional dance and music. All non-fashion primarily conveys an ideal of certainty, and demonstrates a link to a fixed cosmology: this is how we do things, because this is what we know. To have any effect, changes must be absorbed into the abiding scheme. Non-fashion suggests that its wearers have long since settled all fundamental questions and snuffed out the active life of doubt and inquiry; instead, it offers great beauty and originality of form, great subtlety of color and pattern, and many varieties and levels of symbolic meaning refined over generations.

In traditional societies without our sort of uneasy self-propelling fashion, clothing may have immediately readable meaning in its forms, in its methods of wear, and in the character of adornments, all directly linked to the character of customary life, and staying relatively still to do so. Such systems of dress, if they really exist, obviously can make much more accurate social mirrors than fashion ever does; they are not so much representations as direct expressions. Some peasant dress prescribed exact modes for specific social, ceremonial and personal states, with regional differences included in the recipe, so that clothes and other adornments could draw a fairly complete picture of each person's condition throughout life. The formal details had traditional rather than associative sources; they were the same shapes used in the past, and that was itself their whole meaning. Such shapes evolved, although sometimes one or another of them has been stolen from fashionable dress, and then evolved afterwards as if they had always been traditional.

There has moreover always been a great deal of room for individual creative fancy in the productions of traditional societies; we have seen it in rugs and pottery, and the same has been true of dress—which, of course, need not consist of woven cloth. In body-painting societies, pure personal invention might have free reign over one day's overall body pattern, while ritual requirements would strictly govern the one for the next day. In still other cultures, one group of scars on a girl's face showed that she had passed the menarche, while another array of them on her chest was purely ornamental.

In cultures with clothes, the clothes themselves might form a kind of family possession, each garment being transmissible to the next generation and never intended merely for one person, even when it was first made. The similarities of dress binding the entire group reflected common self-awareness and common memory; but difference in individual psychological flavor was also given scope. You could choose your own colors for the ribbons and the petticoats, and embroider your stomacher with fanciful variety, so people could judge your taste; but you always wore the correct number of skirts and the right form of headdress, so people would know your village, whether you were married, and whether you were dressed for work or church.

Such schemes for dress did exist in Europe and elsewhere, although most of them have become obsolete. In Europe, they were perhaps even hastened to their death by the move to preserve them that began in Romantic times and ended with a reductive version of "traditional costume" being falsely congealed into a theatrical uniformity and mass-produced, mainly for the sake of display to outsiders. Folk dress has no more real life in the West, because the modern representational impulse is so strong and so desirable.

Westerners feel the need for references in pictures and mirrors, the image-making requirement that forbids unselfconsciousness; the peasant or ethnic picture was originally made without reference to other images. It was itself the artless work of art, and no mirror was needed to check its effects except the helping hands and eyes of others in the group. There is plenty of dress that is still like this, including mutilation and scarification, in parts of Asia, Africa, and South America; but the more attractive modern idea has swept much of it away.

This has happened because people in many traditional societies have obviously wanted it so. Western fashion offers a visual way out of the trap of tradition, the prison of unquestioning wisdom. Fashion allows clothing to create an image of skepticism, of comic possibility, of different powers and alternative thoughts, of manifold chances, of escape from fixed meanings and fixed roles. Thus modern fashion has consistently looked wonderful from a distance, especially to young people seeking change from old ways. The internal view, on the other hand, is often charged with ambivalence.

In fashion, all social facts about the wearer can theoretically be masked except for personal taste, and even that may be suppressed at will for politic ends. Nevertheless people uneasily realize that the unconscious sources of personal taste in modern fashion can make it convey a whole spectrum of social and personal information much like what is straightforwardly offered in traditional dress, only unconsciously instead of on purpose. Besides that, the social laws that govern choice in fashion are both unwritten and slippery, and wearing the right thing requires the right instinct and judgment instead of plain obedience to the rules of custom. Thus in modern fashion, everything with private meaning for the individual, the whole combination of conscious and unconscious forces that create a personal decision about what to wear at a given time (especially a taste for modishness) can take on the air of being a nasty secret, whose exposure compromises the wearer as the wearers of ethnic dress never are compromised. People who fear the work of fashion are likely to sneer at it, in favor of what seem like the refreshingly honest displays of traditional dress.

While its true purpose is creative, fashion has been wrongly thought to exist just to make people tell lies, to conceal or display things for bad reasons, one bad reason supposedly being that everyone else is doing it; and fashion thus begins to seem like a kind of poison or disease. Dickens and other moralistic novelists have been ferociously hostile toward old women dressing fashionably, for example, as if they were lying about their age, or toward lower-class women knowing how to dress elegantly, as if they were lying about their origins. The important imaginative function, the spiritually enlarging character of fashion, is often blindly ignored so as to paint fashion as wicked, just as novels were once forbidden for being mere falsehoods.

The psychological effort involved in making fashionable choices is indeed repellent to many. Social demands that require making them have sometimes been seen as infringements of liberty, as if a greater liberty really resided in the peasant or non-modern system, where a few simple rules are followed that everyone in the group respects, personal choice has the same very limited scope for everyone, and unconscious revelations are minimal. People uncomfortable with taking full responsibility for their own looks, who either fear the purely visual demands of social life—"appearance" or "appearances"—or don't trust the operation of their own taste, feel threatened and manipulated by fashion, and have called it a tyrant. The constant element of fiction in it makes it smack of inauthenticity, pretense and pretention; and it is indeed obvious that fashion is a perpetual test of character and self-knowledge as well as taste, whereas traditional dress is not.

In the fashion-clad West, traditional costume has consequently been viewed with envy, amazed admiration and often condescendingly exaggerated respect. Cruel displays that permanently mutilate have aroused contempt and fear; but those kinds of cosmetic and elegant arrangement are apparently thought of as absolutely different from lovely saris and kimonos. The stable, fashion-free beauty of much traditional clothing has indeed been assumed to demonstrate a superior quality of social and personal being, and a superior level of esthetic achievement. Some people have been eager to believe that its forms never change, just like the cycles of nature, and that Middle Eastern dress, for example, hasn't altered for thousands of years.

But the truth is that the volatile, nervy visual thrusts and parries of fashion created a true esthetic advance, a cultural leap analogous to other forward moves in the history of Western art, commerce and thought— polyphony and perspective, double-entry bookkeeping and the scientific method, to name some—that have sustained the life and breath of the West. It has only been from the advantageous position all these have afforded that Westerners have felt free to sneer at them all, and at fashion along with them, and to elevate the productions created by more limited worlds, just as they have elevated the workings of harsh nature itself.

WESTERN MEN have apparently felt inadequate to the fullest possible range of fashion for many generations—roughly since 1800, when Romantic Western views of nature came into focus right along with Romantic views of folk dress. As a result, they have even gradually appeared to create a sort of fake traditional dress out of male fashion, almost a pseudo-ethnic costume, something with well-classified and very limited esthetic demands that commands general respect and avoids unfettered personal fantasy—something that can look, sneakily and falsely, like non-fashion. But let's not be fooled; it's still only an anti-fashion fashion, like many others we've seen.

The extraordinary persistence of classic male tailoring for nearly two centuries, during a period of extreme social upheaval and scientific advance, has prompted several possible explanations, some of which I intend to explore later. But one looks immediately all too easy: J. C. Flügel called it "the Great Masculine Renunciation." The idea is that when fashion became very flighty at the end of the eighteenth century, men simply quit, as if in protest.

Another limited way of describing this has been to say that men made a cowardly retreat from both the risks and the pleasures of fashion, and that their dress has ever since been something of a bore. A hasty view of male and female fashion since 1800 could easily yield the false idea that men have largely stayed out of the game until the late twentieth century; and a hostile view of feminine fashion might suggest that they did it to propose an alternative and superior way of doing things, to create a living visual objection to the extreme demands that fashion can make. Women, naturally, could then be despised for meeting them.

Late in this century, some women began publicly to agree with such possible objections, and their agreement has often taken the form of religiously copying the male scheme and deploring the female one. Certain feminists in the 1970's boasted that they did not own a skirt, as if to announce a withdrawal from fashion altogether, the way men had been believed to do. The truth is that men have never abandoned fashion at all, but have simply participated in a different scheme. Men's tailored clothes have been amazingly variable and expressive since 1800, fully as fluid and imaginative as women's modes; but they have consistently appeared in opposition to the feminine method, which has effectively put them in the shade.

All the components of male tailored clothing have varied in shape and texture, scope and behavior. Coats have been boxy and short, fitted and long, with differing dispositions of button and trim; trousers have been wide and soft, stiff and narrow, pegged or flared. Coats and pants have been made of separate fabrics, or of the same one. Waistcoats, lately in eclipse but now in revival, have steadily varied, often colorfully, constantly changing their formal relation to the rest of the suit; and the whole flavor of the tailored male has been alternatively sleek or rough, pliant or rigid, amiable or forbidding. Extraordinarily various styles of collar and tie have come in and out of fashion, changing form and connotation; and variably casual versions of neckwear have accompanied more formal arrangements. Especially interesting has been the stylistic variability of hats, those great male emblems dating from the remote past. Formal hats are lately in abeyance; informal ones are flourishing as never before. Styles in men's clothes have merged, separated and rejoined, constantly creating new ideas of what looks right and what doesn't, all within the same flexible convention; and the elegant masculine mixture has moreover been endlessly enriched from inelegant sources. Men's gear may have looked like non-fashion, but that is a complete illusion; its commitment to risk and irony is just as deep as that of the feminine mode, and its representational character just as strong.

Modern male fashion has in fact been an impressive achievement in modern visual design, since it has used an established set of formal rules, rather like the Classical orders of architecture, while flowing along at the same rate of constant change as women's dress. Like other aspects of modern design, it has been an important illustration of modern views and feelings, as fashion is agreed to be, and not a retreat from them. Trends in modern feminine fashion have in fact supported this idea, as women have increasingly used bits of male garb for every common purpose, often adopting outmoded elements that men have currently abandoned, but that still lie within the modern canon and still visually satisfy. Women's fashion, so noticeable, so "Fashionable," has often been used to show how interesting male fashion really is.

FEELINGS OF DISMAY about the whole of fashion have been expressed since its very beginning. These have taken the form of objections to its morally or esthetically outrageous looks, and to the expensive and inconvenient character of its changes, but even more to its requirement that people of both sexes pay constant attention to their physical appearance. It is nevertheless curious to note that fashion began its robust, long life in medieval Christian Europe, right along with religious and intellectual ideals elevating the mind and spirit far above the flesh and the material world. It is clear that in such a climate the charm of fashion would always lie in its treacherous unconscious operation, its necessary visualization of fantasies otherwise not expressed; and that once in motion, fashion would therefore be as much feared and reviled and despised as followed. The anti-fashion literature is enormous, thunderous, scathing and centuries old.

MEANING IN FASHION

WITHOUT THE EXCUSE of traditional usage, the most vivid forms in fashion cry out for social interpretations in current history. But since the forms have mostly unconscious sources which are veiled from current awareness, the social meaning can really only be adduced later and projected backward to account for particular phenomena. And then, as with so much else, it is easy to interpret incorrectly from the standpoint of a different historical time, to miss something or add something. But in any case, what is said at the time must be taken with deep reservations. People may now say, for example, that the huge female shoulder-padding of the 1980's, which is going out of fashion in the nineties, showed that women wanted to imitate the appearance of male strength. But during the rise of the fashion, nobody following it could admit such a thing, and the new attractiveness of the look had to be accounted for by more appealing-sounding reasons—it makes waists look smaller, for example. And so it does, but that's not enough to explain it, any more than a direct imitation of male deltoids is.

A recent past that includes a strong feminist movement makes this sort of interpretation seem easy and satisfying, since the social facts and the fashionable changes can both be dated, and a link asks to be made. But since we may be obviously misled about the unconscious motivations behind the fashions of earlier days, and read our modern preoccupations into them just when we think we are seeing them most clearly, we may learn from this that we can also be wrong about our own recent past. We are always wrong to find simple answers, if we are really searching for the significance of form.

One problem is that much of what appears in clothing simply won't lend itself to the easy kind of meaning that big shoulders can suggest. Many funny-looking things in fashion clearly have sources that are unfathomable, and that fact makes even the easy answers seem doubtful. Some motifs can be readily explained by fashion's conscious allusion to some specific image, such as the looks of certain actors or singers, or athletes or rulers, or persons representing a country or a cause in the news. But what about the mad vogue for a certain shape of collar, the placement of pockets, a way of lacing shoes, or the style of caps? What might these have to do with current psychological dispositions? Who starts it and why do others love it? Why, indeed, do only some others love it?

There are again only partial answers to these questions, either in the canny inventiveness of commercial designers or in the huge fleeting popularity of groups and public figures. Waves of sartorial desire sweep over certain portions of the public, and observers must marvel before they even try to analyze. Most of it I would insist is a desire for the shape or form itself, not for expressing any meaning by it; the love of its looks is enough, and modern assumptions about art and design support such love. Love for a particular form is engendered by the slackening of keen desire for an earlier form, a sort of esthetic lassitude that is often unconscious, and becomes conscious only when a new form is offered. Since the ideal of formal change has been internalized, any form must arise, flourish, and sink; but in the subversive flow of fashion, we invent something new to like before we acknowledge that we are sick of the old.

Those big female shoulders of the eighties were often worn with androgynous-looking pants and short hair, supporting the idea of masculine imitation; but they were simultaneously worn with full manes of hair, short tight skirts and high heels. Both formulations seem to have more to do with old and new media imagery and with the state of form in fashion during the preceding epoch than with aspects of feminism. With respect to fashion's constant change of bodily shape, big shoulders

were much in need of revival, having been long eclipsed; and their earlier manifestation, retrievable from old movies, went with short skirts
and long hair, not long pants and shingled hair. The latter phenomena,
however, could be seen on the *men* in old movies, who can now be imitated by women according to a general modern custom of seductively
dressing up in outmoded male gear.

Obviously, both thick curly manes and neatly shingled heads also
needed to reappear in women's fashion, after the sleekly teased mountains and the lank locks so common everywhere in the two decades just
before. Visual changes must depend on what is already there to look at;
they can't seize a meaning from the atmosphere and try to match it with
a shape. In the continuum of fashion, the shape must evolve from the
previous shape, opposing or distorting or confirming it. Whatever form
it takes, it will later be given a meaning that matches the current mental-
ity. Therefore seeing an intrinsic meaning in it, like male strength in big
shoulders, or feminine submission in tight corsets, is probably risky at
any time.

What the immediate meaning usually comes from is available imagery, past or present, the suggestive pictures that have pervaded public consciousness and are loaded with shared associations. But wideness
and narrowness, which have derived both from common imagery and
from unconscious desire to modify earlier kinds of wide or narrow form,
are often wrongly lent such intrinsic meanings. The misguided impulse
to attribute them shows a superstitious belief that fashion is a "primitive" rather than a modern art, a set of visual combinations that are really
consciously coded messages, like those in the peasant village or indeed
on a Pacific Northwest totem pole. In other words, that padded shoulders don't have an authentic place in the history of form, a way of looking in a sequence of such ways; that they *only* have meaning; that they
are to be "read" in a certain way, and not seen for themselves.

To some extent they certainly are signals, since fashions do simply
identify the members of groups who follow them, and those can be reg-
istered by observers. But what makes meaning in modern fashion different from that of totem poles, and of modes of dress that are like them, is
that the basic element in the modern art of dress is the changing image
of the whole clothed body, not a set of individual schematized shapes,

developed to carry common meaning in a unifying vessel. The varying shapes of heel, pocket, and belt are not used as if they were derived from some legendary Wolf, Crocodile or Eagle, combined in a design that combines their legendary force.

The modern clothed body is a complete figural image, cinematic or televisionary in its impact. The details that compose it have little meaning beyond their fleeting place in the picture; it is the whole picture that carries the meaning, if any. The modern art of fashion is always referring to the clothed figure, past and current, as it appears in the illustrative arts that have made fashion intelligible since its early days. It is the illustrative medium in art that makes fashion possible at all. Repeated pictures keep images present in the eye, desirable, ready for associative significance, and prone to instant imitation followed by swift modification, subversion, replacement and eventual rediscovery.

Desirable form in fashion is shown and told in pictures, where the medium can sharpen its edge, swell its curve, polish its surface, underline its fleeting glory. One has to admit that now, for example, without the camera there would be no fashion. But one can also see that at the time of Dürer, for example, the fashionable slump of shoulders and the breathtaking break of folds could not have seemed so modish without his and his colleagues' delicious engravings, which taught elegant people how to see what made them look elegant.

It is not the singer himself, but the thousand pictures of him in the media that bring to life and nourish the vogue for his looks, and modify it and play with it, although his music initially sets the fashion for him. And before the present media, the work of countless illuminators and portrait painters, commercial illustrators, engravers and advertising artists gave fashion its perpetual currency. This is a currency not just of images but of the mode of making them—"realistic," fictional, bound to a dramatic human narrative that is never finished, a modern serial tale. We use the mirror to check our place in it.

And so when Western fashion came into existence in the late Middle Ages, and inaugurated modernity in dress to match the other modernities emerging at the same period, it began the process that has finally put all modern clothing (not just the trappings of the rich and idle, who merely began the idea) into the representational mode. To do that, it needed the help of the new realistic representations in art, which had achieved a stunning perfection by the fifteenth century. Then, the swift spread of printed images after 1500 could set visual standards for dress, and support the idea that an actual clothed figure is most desirable when it looks like an ideal realistic picture. Eventually every modern clothed person would create a picture referring to other pictures, and no formal messages could ever again be direct. All modern dress would be like art, with its own rules—even though one of its rules might be to suggest nature and look artless, or to resemble ancient tradition and look timeless. Such effects would last a certain while or fill a certain niche, just like other fashions.

Fashion has thus been able to become a set of illustrations itself. Unlike the peasant or ethnic clothes, it keeps shifting both what and how it illustrates, following all the other modern illustrative arts. Some components may be metaphorical and others direct, some fresh and some fixed in convention; and in fashion, all these shift around over time, taking the body with them. The general idea of subversion remains fundamental. The idealizing, normative impulse must always be undermined and the drama pursue its next act, small or large, often accompanied by a certain amount of scandal. But this has no entirely predictable way of happening, and no fixed schedule, because that, too, would produce a stability foreign to the needs of fashion. Changes moreover occur piecemeal, so that the picture alters when only some parts shift and others endure.

Shifts can't even be shown to follow the changes in society with any temporal exactitude. They are much more likely to precede them, as the unconscious desire for change appears in the illustrative bodily realm before anyone articulates and reasons the need. Each change in fashion's emblem, which is always cast in the form of a clothed figure as a picture, may bring a new arrangement for its illustrative effects, not just a difference in width or length. Width and length may change, but also the style of the picture; and the rhythm at which any of them changes is largely unpredictable. In the case of the masculine tailored suit, hardly any big changes occur, even while history undergoes upheavals and female skirts fly up and down. Small changes therefore look all the more important and get more attention.

Ever since the attention of anthropologists and sociologists was first drawn to modern fashion instead of to traditional dress, they have tried to predict its changes with respect to social change, sometimes claiming that skirt-length will "always" be connected to the movements of the stock market, or that elegant women's waistlines will "always" be displaced after cataclysmic wars; but such rigid rules have not been accurately borne out by later history, and the effort has been given up. One thing they did not predict was the breaking up of fashion into many simultaneous streams, so that wars and stock-market shifts might have multiple and even contradictory visual echoes, or advance flourishes; and the common fashionable scene might gain a new kind of diversity not based simply on class and occupation, but on different imaginative styles often within the same socio-economic group.

The fashion map might even come to resemble what the ethnic map of European folk dress once looked like. We can see how generally the integrative desire in classic modern fashion, exemplified by modern tailoring, has been encroached upon by a new desire for incoherent multiformity, the visual state once thought of as "primitive"—non-modern, peasant-like. The use of many disparate printed patterns in one costume, for example, or the use of many disparate pieces of jewelry at once— some beads, a chain with a cross, another chain. Both these effects, once associated with Gypsies and other unmodern groups, have now become common in urban fashion.

The disintegrative flavor is marked: using many patterns prevents each from showing to advantage. The same is true of disparate ornamentation, or separate conventions used in one costume. The visual result is confusing and unfocussed; and that very result is clearly desired by many at present. Links with the dissolution of the Soviet Union or with the Multicultural Movement, however, must not be forged too rapidly; the currently modish fragmenting impulse already dates back a quarter of a century, when fashion itself broke up into separate living fragments under counter-cultural pressure, and disintegrated dress simply became one possibility among others.

FORM AND SEXUALITY

MODERN DESIRE is subversive. Modern fashion, acting as the illustrator of modern civilization's discontents, never tries to tame collective fantasy into a fixed shape meant to last, but is always prodding it, urging it to keep on making awkward new suggestions instead of repeating fine old assertions. In literary fictions, modern need moves away from the comfort of repetitive incantation and saga toward compact lyric and the phrasing of vivid and disturbing personal narrative; and the same applies in the visual domain.

Whenever the chief desire of the eye is a reliance on immemorial forms, the prevailing esthetic spirit isn't modern. For visual satisfaction, modernity requires conflict and dialectic, uneasy combination, ambiguity and tension, irony, the look of dissatisfied search. This means that any clear and stable modern visual harmony, if and when it is achieved, depends on tension and sacrifice, the posture of imaginative vigilance—you can see it in the best works of abstract painting or sculpture and in modern architecture, and you can see it in modern abstract suits. When rightly managed, such balanced and coherent simplicity always looks vibrant and not dull, never static but always charged with potential change—and indeed sexy. Modern simplicity has become one highly erotic theme at play in all forms of design.

For modern clothes, sexuality became the fundamental expressive motor, the underlying source of creative play, of waywardness, of invention including both the practical and the regressive kind: fashion came to portray sexuality itself as lawless, wayward and inventive. All indices of social class and function were contained by the sexual mode, so that men's clothes were always noticeably masculine first, and only afterwards noble, professional, rural, proletarian. Since fashion started, the forms that expounded the male or female body in dress were generated by sexual fantasy and then tempered to suit other dimensions of life. I would emphasize that *sexuality*, which I claim as the foundation for form in fashion, is not the same thing as *seductiveness*. This last has emerged and subsided in fashion for either sex at certain periods; but I would claim that sexuality itself is behind any strong form in fashion whether or not the form calls attention to the sexual characteristics of the wearer. Sexuality, that is, as distinct from any simple differentiation between male and female.

All this only became true when Western fashion got fully under way, somewhere between 1200 and 1400. Elegant clothes during that period, after consisting of the same basic shapes on which ornament provided the interest, began to require padding or constriction for the torso, extreme shortness or trailing length for garments, and carefully wrought, expressive shapes for shoes, sleeves, and headgear—and to keep changing these requirements. There was a new insistence on cut and fit, to shape the torso tightly and sometimes strangely, and then to change the shape. The same period saw a new use of extra fabric to extend the body's visual scope, to create conspicuous and kinetic shapes around it that obviously went against the force of practical need, and well beyond a social need for simple ostentation. Eventually parts of the body might be smoothly packed away, but then referred to on the surface. A woman's bodice, for example, instead of allowing her breasts to form hills under the fabric, would be made to flatten out all her fleshly curves into an abstract cone, which would then be adorned with two semicircular festoons of pearls. These would replace the natural curves of the breasts with a reference suggesting that breasts themselves are ornaments.

This very fashion, originating in sixteenth-century France but apparent at other European courts, is a good example of how pictorial fashion had already become by that time. The style is now known only from painted and engraved portraits, like so many other modes; and it was also undoubtedly promulgated among the noble ladies of Europe by engravings and miniatures in its own time. Only artists could make a bodice so smooth, the chest above so uniformly waxen, shoulders so boneless, and pearls so perfectly draped. Life was undoubtedly already imitating art in the sixteenth century, and the fashion seems to be referring to pictorial conventions stricter than itself. But its power to satisfy lay deeper than that, in the new representational force of fashion, which allowed a retreat from the actuality of breasts into the abstract, emblematic figure dress could make them a part of.

It was with the development of such devices in fashion that dress became a modern art. It began to operate symbolically and allusively through fashionable shape and ornament, using its own suggestive applied forms in a dynamic counterpoint to the shapes of real bodies. Fashion has done this ever since, just as art has done, making its own agreement with natural forms to create a vital sequence in its own medium. But in fashion, of course, part of the medium is always the live person experiencing its life.

In harmony with the other visual arts at the same time, clothing came to propose a three-dimensional and illusionistic program for the clothed body, a new fictional medium, a poetic form, something that conveyed imagined truths with the added status of reported facts, a drama using live actors. The body itself became fictionalized. Persons became figures and characters, not just members of groups. Fashion invented a poetic visual vocabulary to demonstrate, even unconsciously, overlapping and simultaneous themes of temporality and contingency, or social placement and personality, but always cast in the terms of sexuality that are demanded by the living body, hers or his. Competitive dressing came to be based on suggestive changes in shape, color, line and proportion, all with respect to bodily shapes, and on variable piquancy in the forms of ornaments, not just on their value.

As a part of the drama of sexuality, the fiction of fashion began to deal with the idea of phrasing through time, adroitly joining the forces of memory and desire in one picture, framed by awareness of death. The desirable visual mode came to depend on a peculiar difference between a present way to look and an earlier way, not just between silk and homespun, nor between sleek and crude adornment, nor between different symbolic colors, nor even simply between this way and that way of wrapping the same sash. A sense of dramatic sequence, rather than of static apparition, came to underlie the quality of desirable appearance. Rich and poor effects kept their obvious significance, but the representational medium of fashion came to impose its own construction on them, editing any direct meaning they carried. Crudity might be temporarily witty, refinement tacky; and past effects were always to be recycled in new contexts to make detached comment on former taste.

Beauty ceased to be an acknowledged aim of fashion, as it remains in so many non-modern, traditional arts. Beauty in fashion comes always as a sort of vivid surprise, as it often does in the experience of sexual love. In fashion, beauty doesn't result from the confident harmony of known form and material, but from brilliant moments of clarified vision. Such moments may be born of desire, but they are always sustained in art, as I suggested earlier, by vigilance, technique and imagination. Above all, beauty in fashion is constantly created *ad hoc* by the pictorial artists who make a medium for it and convey it everywhere, who can make the beauty of an image seem identical with the beauty of a garment.

Insisting further on the theme of sex, men and women began to dress extremely differently from each other somewhere during the fourteenth century, having worked up to it rather slowly during the two before. After that, the borrowing of visual motifs across a visually sharper sexual divide created more suggestive interest and emotional tension in clothing than it ever could have done when men and women wore similarly designed garments. Small suggestions of transvestism became more noticeable and more exciting.

Art shows how the change worked. In the early Middle Ages until about 1100, when garments for both sexes were still relatively shapeless, relief sculptures and mosaics tended to create one unifying pattern of drapery inside compositions that combined male and female figures. The result was that the clothing seemed to link the sexes instead of dividing them. This scheme for clothes in art derived partly from such Classical monuments as the celebrated *Ara Pacis* of the Emperor Augustus from the early first century A.D., where the frieze of men and women is awash in a rhythmic arrangement of drapery.

This particular Roman drapery seems to clothe everybody in one endless length of fabric, so that determining the sex of any single figure on the frieze requires some scrutiny. But by the later fourteenth century, the ladies in illuminations and paintings are instantly discernible in their high, stiffened veils and long, trailing skirts, which appear in striking contrast to the articulated bodies and bushy hair of the gentlemen. In

ABOVE: Roman bas-relief, *Ara Pacis,* west elevation, Rome, 13–9 B.C. BELOW: Byzantine mosaic, *The Empress Theodora and Retinue,* Ravenna, 500–526 A.D.

Although male and female clothes actually differed, the artists of antiquity and the early Middle Ages showed men and women similarly draped and of similar size and shape. All clothing has been uniformly stylized so as to unite rather than separate the two sexes.

ABOVE: Manuscript illumination, *Le Roman de la violette,* French, mid-fifteenth century. LEFT: Master E.S., engraving, *The Knight and His Lady,* German, mid-fifteenth century.

Vivid new differences between male and female dress characterize the first developments of true fashion, and are emphasized by the artists of the late Middle Ages and the early Renaissance. Male fashion is based on the brilliant bodily articulations of plate armor (left), while female fashion exaggerates the enveloping skirt below with a very small tight bodice above. Men now have flowing curly hair and visibly shapely legs, feet and genitals; women cover the hair and have no visible shape below the waist, but they expose the neck and chest.

keeping with its dynamic emotional core, fashionable clothing began to display not just plain sexual difference, as traditional clothing always does, but a rich form of dramatic adversarial expression between men and women, which is one of the recurrent fictional themes of modernity in general.

In fashion, it is indeed the element of personal story, so important to modern literature and the telling of modern history, that lies behind its temporal style of formal language, behind all the effects that are forced to change so as to conform to temporal phrasing. Unlike anything else in the material world, clothing must deal with each person's body. Many may not wear one garment, as many may shelter under one roof and eat from one pot. But fashion goes still further than clothing, to engage with the idea of an individual body having an individual psyche and a particular sexuality, a unique youth and maturity, a single set of personal experiences and fantasies. This is a notion quite at odds with what the figures on the *Ara Pacis* had been suggesting, or what the whole range of garments worn in the peasant village convey. Fashion is relentlessly personal.

Although it seems to require that many people do the same thing, fashion is nevertheless committed to the idea of unique personality in the very forms it uses—the material forms generated out of unconscious fantasy, which begins in the individual psyche. It is these forms that have always seemed to make fashion ridiculous, and people ridiculous along with it: the peculiar hats, the pointed shoes, the useless appendages, the varieties of constriction, the big shoulders, the whole story; and this has consistently applied to both sexes. Art, modernizing at the same time, shows the same new personal character in the new evocative and suggestive formal vocabulary that infuses the work of the early Renaissance, the three-dimensional curves and shadows that offer compelling personal expositions in Masaccio's frescoes and Van Eyck's panels.

In emphasizing the idea of an individual body, fashion thus illustrates the idea that sexuality, with its reliance on individual fantasy and memory, governs each person's life. It illustrates collective life as if it were personal narrative, with its linear, subjective path through time. By offering extreme visions that seem to satisfy everybody for a minute, but simultaneously to offend and upset everybody, fashion itself refers obliquely to the way lust, fear, or zeal may overwhelm the moment, only to shift with the flux of days and the shift of circumstance. Fright and lust (or contempt, or self-loathing, or hatred) may make people ridiculous for the time being; but they are legitimate conditions everyone respects, especially in the modern world.

Fashion can represent emotional forces that don't have to be the direct echo of any one wearer's feelings during such a fashion's vogue. The fashion will be a collective vision; but it will use the shapes that lie in individual psychic depths, and it will be guided by available imagery in the available arts, using garments people recognize. Thus, in fashion, aggression (or boredom, or hope, or longing for childhood) will seem to be expressed by everybody's clothes for a time, even those who are not feeling those things, because it suits the prevailing temper to acknowledge them and not others in the silent theater of the mode.

By "everybody," I of course mean not really everybody, since there is now no single fashion, nor has there ever really been; but everybody in one visible group. To do this, the curves and angles of dress in several different fashions may unconsciously imitate and mock bodily forms (even lungs and intestines, or teeth and vertebrae) always in direct contact with parts of real bodies, and at the same time use recognizable garments with publicly acknowledgeable sources. The references may make a double mockery, or a doubly remote allusion.

The allusion to known imagery not only gives coherence and an acceptable public meaning to the shapes of fashion, but intervenes to edit and temper their direct effect. The picture creates the enabling distance between the wearer and the direct psychological meaning of the form; if women are actually padding their shoulders to suggest strength, or wearing masses of extremely untidy hair to suggest emotional license, they need not believe it at the time, but only see the desirability of the look as expounded in currently admired images of actresses or models, and approximated by attractive persons in the common world. Explanations of fashion are so often incomplete because the sources for the deep appeal of certain forms and styles must be hidden, in order that fashion may freely do its creative work.

Clothes that are in fashion may make the body refer to parts of itself, and to other clothed versions of itself, and to liken other objects to bodily parts. A certain sort of hat may make a person's head suggest a penis—that's fairly obvious; but other hats can make the head into a sort of fist, a possible foot, a muscle; or they may simply refer to other known hats—a railroad-worker's cap or a sunbonnet. Or, most commonly, both at once. Along with strength, padded shoulders on either sex can also bring breasts and buttocks to mind; certain pants can seem like sleeves, making legs into arms; and many have noticed that a very low-cut shoe turns a woman's instep into a chest or a back in a very low neckline, with suggestive cleavage between the first two toes.

Dressed bodies may be made to resemble bric-a-brac or plants, trash-heaps or sailboats. Strips of fabric anywhere on the body make ghost shackles or notional bandages. A sarong suggesting the South Seas may also seem like a bath towel; it may be worn with a dandified jacket evoking Beau Brummell or with a leather tunic that would go well on a medieval headsman in a thirties movie. Costume jewelry in particular is made for this sort of task, now seeming to offer nice morsels to eat or amusing handles to turn, now instruments of torture or lethal machinery, now arcane badges of office from unknown ancient cults. One style of shirt may suggest terrorism, another an earlier century or a trite fantasy about the future.

Fashion now also offers garments bearing words that play a lexical game with underlying breasts, chests, backs, bellies, and shoulders—in a semiological climate, detachable words have been added to the common stock of visual fantasy, to be mixed with body-parts and picture-parts. Fashion provides modish versions of characters from the visual arts, so that you can dress like Bart Simpson, say; but if you prefer, fashion will also let you wear a picture of Bart Simpson on your chest, or the words "Bart Simpson" instead. You can moreover dress like Van Gogh, or like one of Van Gogh's models, or you can wear a tee-shirt saying "Van Gogh" on it. You can alternatively have Van Gogh's *The Starry Night* embroidered in sequins on the back of your jacket, or his own painted face photoprinted on your leg-warmers.

Fashionable clothes thus always look personal, since the forms composing them refer to individuality, even if the clothes share in the looks of everybody else's at the moment. Fashion indeed owes its extraordinary power to the way it can make each person look truly unique, even while all the people following the mode are dressing very much alike. The deep need to be singular and the deep need to be part of a group are simultaneously fulfilled by fashion—it has always allowed you to have your cake and eat it, if you have the strength of your convictions and faith in your eye.

Even when many people wearing one fashion seem superficially to resemble one another, the suggestive configurations of modish clothing will in fact lend a further individuality to each, as general fashions can't help bringing out certain personal qualities and suppressing others. The same chic short hair will make one man look grim and another man look boyish; and a few years later, chic long hair will make the same grim one look romantic and the boyish one formidable.

NOW, IN THE LAST quarter of this century, women discontented with present aspects of female fashion may simply adopt a different fash ion, one of the several available that are quite unlike the feminine modes of the past. An enlightened woman may prefer to call such clothing Basic, Timeless, Purely Comfortable, and Not Fashion—but of course it still is. Unless she weaves or knits the fabric and invents every bit of the costume out of her head, fashion designers are designing any garments she buys, and the fashion business is making and marketing them, with the same energy it applies to those creations labelled with famous names that are reported in the fashion press.

But it is extremely interesting that when contemporary women wish to be simple and timeless and outside fashion, the clothes they usually choose are traditionally masculine in origin, the pants and shirts and jackets and sweaters of modern classic male dress, jeans and flannel shirts included. Instead of aiming for any purely female basic way to dress, like some of their dress-reforming forbears in the last century, they have simply moved to partake directly of established male fashion, as women have repeatedly shown a desire to do for centuries. In this century, they have succeeded. There is apparently no present escape from women's ancient wish to wear men's clothes, turn them to female account, and to feel liberated when they do it. Why?

There is, I would claim, something perpetually more *modern* about male dress itself that has always made it inherently more desirable than female dress. It is not just the sign of power in the world, or of potency in the head, nor has it ever generally been more physically comfortable; but since the late Middle Ages, male dress also has had a certain fundamental esthetic superiority, a more advanced seriousness of visual form not suggested by the inventors of fashion for women in the past. To discover what that is, we will again have to go back a bit.

EARLY FASHION HISTORY

FIRST, ABOUT BORROWING bits of dress from the other sex. Extremely separate male and female effects in fashion, like those in 1380 or 1680, in 1850 or 1950, suggest that each sex currently wants to have a very clear sense of distance from the other one. Communities have sometimes enforced such sartorial separation with considerable rigor, making laws prohibiting transvestism and imposing stiff penalties for violations. But this usually begins to happen when the visual differences between men's and women's clothes are actually in a new state of confusion, and fashion is beginning to bring the sexes closer together after having sharply divided them. Since it is committed to sexual expression, fashion has repeatedly done this, because sexuality itself gets a sharp specific emphasis if someone uses the clothes of the other sex—especially without otherwise hiding his or her own. It is sexual *pleasure,* set up in visible defiance of the clear male and female signals designed to further procreation, that is emphasized by any hint of homoerotic fantasy in clothes; and it frightens many.

Since personal sexuality is always the engine of fashion, anything erotically disturbing will repeatedly tend to emerge on its surface, in opposition to whatever has lately been conventionally defining males and females. Sartorial borrowings from the other sex, whether individual or collective, suddenly display a modern kind of knowledge that sexuality is fluid, unaccountable and even uncomfortable, not fixed, simple and easy. Besides sex, fashion insists on risk. If the visual divide between men and women starts looking too symbolic, too untroubled, too conventional instead of dramatic, fashion will begin producing an erotic disturbance. But not, of course, always the same one.

It's therefore not surprising that mainstream feminine fashion has so often fed on the surface device of selective borrowing from men, usually in small doses, for provocative effect. But George Sand, wearing a complete man's suit in a period when sexual separateness was very intense, became an erotic icon because she looked even more feminine in her tailored jacket and trousers, not masculine—that is, she looked more sexy. Notably, she did not cut her hair or disguise her full figure: it was not drag, with the aim of illusion. By taking up men's clothes, and having them well fitted to her feminine body, she showed herself to be interested not in female concerns like child-bearing and domesticity, nor in the standard feminine uses of alluring submissiveness, but in a female erotic life that depends on an active imagination, on adventurous and multiform fantasy, the modern sort of sexuality customarily reserved for men. Because when fashion first arrived to make clothing modern, it was men's clothes that provided a field for the expression of adventurous sexual fantasy, not women's.

Modernity has obviously recurred in waves, of which only the latest is associated with the beginning of this century. Looking just at clothing since 1200, you can see that spurts of cultural advance were illustrated by the art of dress in sharp new visualizations of human looks, and that most of these were initially masculine. Women's dress reacted to new masculine sartorial assertions both with counter-assertions of exaggerated conservative and submissive elements, and more superficially with theft, especially after about 1515. Women's modes thereafter began to raid bits of male clothing as a standard ploy, an imaginative advance on extreme feminine devices. Things rarely went the other way. It's clear that the fastest and sexiest advances in Western costume history were made in male fashion, including the initial leap into fashion itself in the late twelfth century, the shift into modernity which threw down the challenge to all succeeding generations.

UNTIL THEN, the European scheme for costume since late antiquity had dressed men and women in similar bag-like garments without curved seams, either for armholes or to create any fit around the body.

Three-dimensionality was not built into the construction of the garment, but came into existence as the fabric fell around the wearer and was variously wrapped, belted and fastened. This sort of dress was and still is common to much of the Eastern hemisphere, in societies that do not traditionally have our sort of fashion. And in recent attempts to emulate Western dress, the people of Nepal, for example, follow the ancient rule—it is the men who strive for modernity and now wear cut and sewn Western clothes, while the women keep to the old draperies once worn by both.

During the early Middle Ages men's tunics might sometimes be shorter than women's, but both sexes wore draped clothing still fundamentally like those of the ancient Greeks and Romans, who had also allowed men shorter tunics for active war, active labor and active leisure. Men wore long gowns, too, on all formal civil occasions. The main new medieval difference between the sexes was that with their shorter tunics, men wore separate leg-coverings loosely drawn up and attached to a waistband, and loose-fitting underpants tied around under those, both arrangements well adapted to the European climate and deriving from the original Northern and Northeastern invaders of the Mediterranean world. For Greeks and Romans, they had originally had the potent chic of the forbidden, the outrageous dress of the enemy. Women's stockings, almost invisible, only came up to the knee, and women had no pants at all, even underneath. Some men's clothing thus already formed a somewhat more detailed bodily envelope than women's, even though it was all made of baggy drapes.

Art of the early Middle Ages shows how artists virtually created the beauty of early medieval clothing, inventing beautiful reciprocities of fold, fastening, texture and layer in harmony with stylized arms and legs, combining the components of the figure with abstractions of drapery just as Greek sculptors and vase-painters had done. Early medieval carvers, painters, illuminators and mosaicists were clearly more gifted for couture than the straight-cutting, straight-sewing tailors of the time. You can see modern fashion lurking in the works of art, getting ready to be born.

The first revolutionary advances in European fashion, however, were connected to the late-twelfth-century development of plate armor, which still later male fashions hastened to imitate in various ways. And although subsequent male fashion might exaggerate, compress, decorate and overburden a man's body, and wholly cover its surface, the aim of the design thereafter was nevertheless to expound the male human shape itself. The new development in armor was quite different from the style of Classical armor, which had followed the forms of the ideal nude torso and parts of the arms and legs, coating naked muscles in metal sculpture that seemed to imitate them, and leaving other parts bare.

By contrast, the dynamic formal ingenuity of medieval plate armor suggests that it was designed to enhance the articulated beauty of complete male bodies very creatively, in the modern way, with an invented abstract imagery of multifaceted brilliance and unearthly-looking strength. It was a great esthetic as well as practical advance: early medieval armor had been made of chain mail, which hung straight down like fabric, only heavily and doubtless painfully. Colored tunics were worn over it for dash and glitter as well as identification, and thick tunics underneath for protection from it; but in itself it had no way to enhance the fighting man's figure.

Innovations in armor mark the first real modernity in Western fashion, showing ways to redesign all the separate parts of the male body and put them back together into a newly created shape, one that replaced the naked human frame with another one that made a close three-dimensional, line-for-line commentary on it in another medium. Male clothing lost the unfitted character it had had since antiquity and began to suggest interesting new lines for the torso, and to consider the whole shape of legs and arms in its tailoring scheme. Plate armor moreover required an undergarment made by a linen-armorer, a close-fitting padded suit that outlined the whole man and protected him from his metal casing, of which it followed the shape. Male fashion quickly aped the shapes created by the linen-armorers, who can really count as the first tailors of Europe.

From this time on, round about 1300, clothed men and women began to look extremely different. For men, perfectly fitted tights and tight-fitting doublets were laced together around the waist for smooth overall fit, and formal coats worn over this were very short, neat and padded. Sleeves were also cut of several pieces, shaped, and padded. The separate hose were sewn together to become tights, and drawn up firmly to hide the underpants; and once legs showed all the way up, the codpiece was invented, and padded. In Italy, home of the first Classical revival, some of this articulation clearly echoed the new vogue for the antique male nude, which was also making appearances in Italian Renaissance art; but it was the startling and prestigious beauty of the armed man that most profoundly affected European fashion for centuries afterwards. Most fourteenth-, fifteenth-, sixteenth-, and early-seventeenth-century male dress tended to imitate armor in forming stiff abstract shapes around the body, finally culminating in the starched ruff at the neck, a kind of armor-like abstraction of the shirt collar.

In the same period of European history, women's clothes stayed essentially conservative, relinquishing very little, keeping to the original Classical formulas. Later women's fashion, specifically for erotic effect as we have suggested, often copied masculine *accessories,* not the whole costume. This was one feminine method for quick fashionable variety in what had been generally a slow stylistic progress up to the fifteenth century, during which the elaborate development of sleeved and fitted dresses had only gradually created feminine clothes with more shape and flair than antiquity had provided. Then, after the early sixteenth century, certain female styles of bodice, hat, collar, shoe, and sleeve were simply stolen from men, to add a new whiff of sexual daring to women's clothes without recourse either to forbidden pants or to excessive exposure. Such gestures do not aim for a real masculine effect, the look of active power; they show a desire to look erotically imaginative without looking too feminine—to mimic male sexual freedom, instead of exaggerating the look of female compliance. The whores in Urs Graf engravings of around 1514 wear their male hats with fine provocation, like Marlene Dietrich in her topper.

If Joan of Arc had appeared in male dress and male armor two hundred and fifty years earlier than she did, or one hundred and fifty years later, she might have shocked nobody by her clothes alone. But in the 1420's, her men's clothing was all the more outrageous because men's clothes were so sexually expressive. Joan was violating the strongly divided rule for fashion at the moment; the dragging skirts and tall hair-concealing headdresses of women had become much more emphatic, after men's clothes had begun to follow the lines of their bodies, to show off the complete shapes of their legs, to adopt remarkable footgear and sport their natural hair in interesting styles.

Because of the new element of divided sexual fantasy in dress, Joan looked immodestly erotic in her men's gear. She wasn't just disguised as a man, and she didn't just look soldierly and practical, especially since in her private moments without armor she was something of a dandy. At court, she seized the male privileges of going bareheaded and showing off her legs and figure with attractive tailoring, abandoning the excessively romantic modesty of current women's dress without hiding the fact that she was a woman. The result was that she seemed to be shamelessly displaying the breadth and richness of her sexual fantasies, not simply clothing her spiritual and political strength in its suitable armor. And in so doing, she clearly aroused the sexual fantasies of others. She always insisted on the necessity of her men's clothes, but she never once said they were convenient or comfortable. It all seemed to sort very ill with her spiritual ambition, and helped give her the reputation of sorceress and whore.

FOR CENTURIES after the male revolution in the Middle Ages, women continued to wear variations of the dress, which was simply the same floor-length tunic of antiquity, the chiton, peplos or stola, which had then been worn with a large draped shawl used as overgarment and veil. The dress was traditionally one-piece from neck to hem, but in the Renaissance it came to be made in two sections, so that the top part, the body or bodice, could be stiffened to rhyme with the male fashions based on armor. The dress was worn with a chemise under it and (for the prosperous) a fine long robe over it for formal occasions. With this went some sort of hood, veil or kerchief on the head, symbolically if not actually covering the hair, just as in the ancient world. In cold Europe, the main difference from Mediterranean antiquity lay in the creation of close-fitting sleeves, so that the dress always covered the arms and the overgarment became a sleeved robe instead of the shawl-like drape of Greece and Rome. Sleeves, richly trimmed or not, were sometimes made separately like stockings, slipped up the arm, and laced or pinned in place.

After the dress became two-pieced in the early sixteenth century, its skirt might be a truly separate garment, most commonly called in English a petticoat. This skirt would show behind the opening of the overdress, or below it if the overdress were hitched up. Poor women might only wear a chemise, a petticoat and a sleeveless bodice, or even no bodice; but they would certainly wear a kerchief on the head. The petticoat was originally not an undergarment at all, but simply any separate skirt. As such, it became the one defining female garment, along with the veil for the head. To dress as a woman, in such a way as to be wholly transformed and disguised, all a man needed was a skirt and a kerchief. Right now these two garments will still do it—but only in Western countries.

The female costume stayed essentially the same since the Middle Ages, with eventual changes in the fitting and stiffening of the various parts of it, each of which gave temporary variation to the overall shape and harmonized with male stiffness. But the basic scheme of single undergarment (the chemise, or smock, or shift), long dress, overdress and headdress was of great antiquity and great sobriety, freighted with centuries of symbolic female modesty reaching back to the ancient world. Sleeves were always long, and originally all necklines were high. Once it began, fashion might thicken or thin out the female formula, sometimes imitating the simplicity of the poor, sometimes adding more display with extreme extensions or extra details, sometimes imitating men's accessories; but the scheme was not radically challenged until this century.

The continuity of the formula was of utmost importance, expressing the idea that fashion might keep changing, but that women remained guardians of basic assumptions, embodied principally in the universal long clothes of ancient times that men of the late Middle Ages had felt free to abandon. The refinement of the civil arts seemed to be given over to women, as long gowns became ever more exceptional and ceremonial for men. Men's new armor-like suits set the vigorous, modernizing tone for fashionable change, and set the example, giving women's dress the chance to take opposing or harmonizing shapes, to engage in the new visual dialogue of the sexes, but without abandoning anything at all.

The female image was thus perpetually founded on its own ancient past, varying its basic structure only well within the ancient rules. These had been based on ancient divine law and civil laws; and they easily took on the aura of natural law, so that when long skirts, long hair and requisite head coverings were finally given up by the women of this century, the change seemed like a profound blasphemy. Trousers, of course, were a worse one.

During the history of fashion, one can see the hidden form of the actual woman being virtually replaced by a satisfactory image of the Dressed Woman, often shaped to give her bizarre proportions according to shifts in erotic imagination as fashion kept changing, but always essentially meant to conceal her body in the ancient way, and to replace its plain facts with satisfying mythic and fictional verities. The original expressive aim of ancient female dress had been modesty, as it still is in Islam. Opposing notions of sexual attractiveness were added by fashion, in a tense counterpoint to the original principle of concealment.

Female fashion's first variation on the ancient theme of modesty was the lowering of the neckline in the fourteenth century. When he acquired more noticeable legs, she immediately acquired more noticeable breasts. This was an electrifying maneuver, accomplished without giving up the overlapping draperies that women had worn for millennia, and it was later followed by the equally electrifying stiffening of the bodice, of which one sexy effect was its imitation, as we have said, of the new effects of male armor. These female moves were certainly not independently modernizing steps; if anything they were somewhat regressive, adding an erotic narcissism to modest garments—a dimension that only emphasized their continuity. But the opening of the neckline set a precedent for feminine fashion: ever since the first medieval move toward décolletage, selective exposure of skin was to be a female theme. Although men got to be consistently more innovative with regard to overall tailoring, the whole surface of their bodies was usually covered.

Until the late seventeenth century, the modish costume for both sexes was often distracting and mobile in itself, parts of it puffed out, trailing or swinging, or elaborately embellished on the surface to draw attention away from the actual body and toward all the possibilities of fantasy; but even though male fashion might be tight and heavy, cumbersome and elaborate, the shapes of masculine dress always continued to articulate the body, to demonstrate the existence of a trunk, neck and head with hair, of movable legs, feet and arms, and sometimes genitals—

whereas those of feminine dress did not. The true structure of the female body was always visually confused rather than explained by fashion. It held to the old insistence on female corporeal concealment, now offered by means of imaginative distraction and illusion.

A woman's arms and head might be fairly intelligible, but her hair was usually carefully bound up and often covered by headgear that further disguised the actual shape of her head and its normal relationship to her neck, besides editing the character of her hair itself. Her pelvis and legs were always a mystery, her feet a sometime thing, and her bosom a constantly changing theatrical presentation of some kind. Needless to say, her exposed hands were always dramatic costume elements, exciting bare episodes in a sea of fabric.

On the other hand, the design of male dress had a foundation in the structure of the whole physical body, a formal authenticity derived from human corporeal facts. Its fictions, although also given to deception and illusion, consequently had a more forceful reality than the fantasies of women's modes, especially during the long period of male license for color, invention and display.

Public attention has nevertheless always been rivetted on the feminine scheme of varying the same idea in different ways through time. This has been what is meant by "Fashion" when it is despised as woman's business. The perpetual insistence on using the themes of modesty and eroticism together has provided a fascinating show, and has forever linked the idea of female fashion with falsity. But it is important to remember that despite all the differences in the ways male and female dress were formally conceived, the two sexes created a harmonious visual balance for hundreds of years, as we can see in works of art. Colors and fabrics and trimmings were similar for both sexes, and differed according to station in life and occasion, and sometimes region, but not gender; and the same was true about the degree of complexity and adornment.

One reason for this, and for everything we have so far described, was that all tailors for both sexes were men. The basic scheme for fashion was the product of a male craft, a display conceived as a two-sexed unit, a single visual illustration of the relation between men and women. Tailors moreover existed at all levels of society like cobblers and tinkers; it was not just the rich who had their clothes made. I would also hasten to emphasize that a tailor's female clients would have just as much creative say in his results as male ones would; tailors were humble artisans and not prestigious designers. The choice of colors, details and accessories was certainly a client's own business, man or woman; but the technical standard of design and construction was the same for both sexes, in the village or the city.

LATER CHANGES

GIVEN THE WAYWARDNESS at the core of fashion, we can see that any change in fashion must aim to create a new disequilibrium just when a vivid style has achieved a state of balance and become too easy to take. Contrary to folklore, most changes are not rebellions against unbearable modes, but against all too bearable ones. Tedium in fashion is much more unbearable than any sort of physical discomfort, which is always an ambiguous matter anyway; a certain amount of trouble and effort is a defining element of dress, as it is of all art.

In the past, stiffness, heaviness, constriction, problematic fastenings, precarious adornments and all similar difficulties in clothing would constantly remind privileged men and women that they were highly civilized beings, separated by exacting training, elaborate education and complex responsibilities from simple peons with simple pleasures, burdens and duties. Changes in very elegant fashion usually meant exchanging one physical discomfort for another; the comfort of such clothes was in the head, a matter of honor and discipline and the proper maintenance of social degree.

One basic modern need is to escape the feeling that desire has gone stale. Fashion therefore depends on managing the maintenance of desire, which must be satisfied, but never for too long. It's easy to see how one

LEFT: François Clouet, *Le Duc d'Alençon,*
French, 1575. BELOW: Sánchez Coello,
Queen Anne of Austria, Spanish, c. 1575.

His costume retains the stiffness of armor. The painting, using a plain backdrop, emphasizes his separate parts and their well-defined, wrinkle-free shapes; even the regular folds of his ruff have a metallic rigidity. Below, her collar and hat copy the male fashion, and so does her armor-like bodice; but her costume retains the traditional female formula of underdress and overdress, the sleeves of one showing under those of the other. The overdress has a front opening, here worn closed but much emphasized with braid and big knots.

general impulse of fashion would therefore be, for example, to make the whole body seem rigid when it had been flexible for a long time, as in the case of the armor-like garments of the Renaissance, or to reclarify the anatomical scheme, as Neo-classic fashion did when Baroque and Rococo dress had been blurring its outlines for several generations. An intermediate example appeared in the first half of the seventeenth century, which inaugurated the fashionable impulse to make existing formal schemes more casual, to create an air of accident, of unbalance, even of carelessness or perversity in the choice and wearing of familiar garments. Again, men were responsible, and women's clothes followed their example up to a point.

By 1650, armor had definitively proved itself obsolete in the field and had even lost much of its ceremonial importance; vestigial metal gorgets and breastplates might continue as badges of rank. But during the harrowing period of the Thirty Years' War and the English Civil War in the first half of the seventeenth century, the most exciting fighting man was the rough-and-ready soldier, clad in baggy breeches and a loose-fitting leather jerkin. Under this he wore a plain shirt with huge sleeves, of which bits and snatches showed through the flaps and slits in the jerkin, and the whole figure was covered in straps, buckles and buttons for attaching bits of military gear. He was accoutered with big boots, big hat, big cape and a loosely slung sword.

To echo the flavor, elegant men grew their hair long and affected swagger, loosened their collars and let their stockings wrinkle, and wrapped themselves in sweeping cloaks. An unbuttoned guard-room spirit acquired an aristocratic chic, as the English court portraits by Van Dyck or the French engravings by Jacques Callot amply show. Tight doublets and starched ruffs, clipped hair, neat footwear and padded breeches all began to look ridiculous instead of orderly and imposing. The power of perfect symmetry and containment gave way to the force of impulse and persuasion. There was, in harmony with this new Baroque mode, a general "delight in disorder," the first sartorial display of attractive nonchalance.

In the later twentieth century, we have seen a recurrence of the desire to wear open-collar or collarless shirts and abandon the necktie, to leave the hair uncut and let it flow or flop, to let stubble grow on the chin, to wear unfitted new versions of formerly tight garments, to wear unmatching versions of what used to match, and to adopt the gear of leisure moments for standard dress wear. The conscious, verbal justification of such moves is always easy; they are associated with individual freedom, honesty, and physical comfort in the face of what are suddenly seen as rigid strictures. But they are usually undertaken in fashion's abiding spirit of esthetic subversion—they are active moves toward change for its own sake, not outraged retreats from the iron demands of the mode itself. Fashion is just as severe about ease as it is about order, and loosely knotted scarves and the right degree of stubble are often much harder to manage than formal neckties and smooth shaving.

Given the long-lasting habit of conservatism in female dress, it is not surprising that the instigation of such subversive shifts, such wholesale "modernizations," should have been masculine. Although the details of women's clothing changed during these periods to echo the prevailing flavor, whether of ease or of discipline, women's dress never abandoned the décolleté dress with deceptive skirt and shaping bodice, and the elaborate headdress involving a goodly head of artfully arranged hair, its adornments often including a hood or a veil, a lace or linen cap, or a concealing bonnet, all variations on the same modest idea. Fashionable *hats* were always informal, rakish, slightly indecent for women, since all hats were either masculine or lower-class in origin.

Military costume went on to undergo many changes, and to be the source for much of the male sexuality expressed in dress ever since—to which women have continued to help themselves for interesting effects. The most recent version of the theme has not been military but athletic, with the influence of possible uses for synthetic fibers in the gear for hockey-players, skin-divers, runners, cyclists of all kinds, and racing-car drivers, but also for others who pit their bodily strength against huge odds. Male fashion takes note of mountaineers and astronauts, even extraterrestrials and travellers into the future—gamblers with the fate of the earth, as armed knights and crusaders were perceived to be in the Middle Ages. Armor-like clothing, now often made of synthetic fibers and molded plastic as well as leather, is once again sensational.

During the early-nineteenth-century wave of modernity represented by the famous Dandy mode, which we will later look at in detail, the stylistic source was also more sporting than military, founded chiefly on English country wear for hunting and shooting; and the mode itself was duly imitated in women's clothes, although not for anything other than riding clothes until this century. Until then, also, all elegant female imitations of male dress, military or not, were confined to the upper body except for shoes. The ancient skirt, which hid women from the waist down and thus permitted endless scope for the mythology of the feminine, had become a sacred female fate and privilege, especially after it became firmly established as a separate garment. Men did not wear skirts, although they might wear robes and gowns on occasion.

Trousers for respectable women were publicly unacceptable except for fancy dress and on the stage, and they were not generally worn even invisibly as underwear until well on in the nineteenth century. At that period the common adoption of underpants by women seems to represent the first expression of the collective secret desire to wear pants, only acceptably brought out on the surface with the bicycling costumes of the 1890's, and only finally confirmed in the later twentieth century with the gradual adoption of pants as normal public garments for women.

Anomalous persons like George Sand and Joan of Arc made their temporary sensations in a virtual vacuum; a few movements like that of Amelia Bloomer in the nineteenth century came and went. Pants were still a forbidden borrowing from the male, so unseemly that they could only be generally hidden until their time finally came. After those millennia of dresses, dividing the legs of respectable women with a layer of fabric seemed like sexual sacrilege. Consequently pants on women figured, naturally enough, in soft-core pornography since the eighteenth century, and they were often worn for seductive purposes by fast ladies in elegant society ever since the sixteenth. Trousers had certainly been worn by female mine-workers, fisherfolk and agricultural laborers, and naturally by dancers and acrobats, and actresses or singers in "breeches" parts; but the low status of all these female occupations kept women's pants firmly associated with lowness in general, or else with the Mysterious East, which had its own dubious associations.

The twentieth-century modernization of women was altogether a laggard development, since it came a hundred years later than the great innovations, created for men by English tailors, that still form the basis of modern male dress. At that period, just as with plate armor only better, the male body received a complete new envelope that formed a flattering modern commentary upon its fundamental shape, a simple and articulate new version that replaced the naked frame, but this time without encasing it, upholstering it, stiffening it, or overdecorating it. The modern suit, although it still hid every inch of skin, now skimmed the surface and moved in counterpoint to the body's movement, making a mobile work of art out of the combination.

At that same time female fashion was also temporarily pared down, thinned out and simplified; but it continued throughout the next hundred years with the primitive, disguising long-dress-and-careful-head-dress formula. Fashion was still steadily rearranging the proportions of the female body and avoiding much reference to its actual composition, just as female costume had been doing ever since the first big trailing skirts of the fourteenth century. Nineteenth-century fashionable changes for women became even more distracting on the surface, as the changes in men's clothes continued to be a matter of subtly altering the basic tailored shape and its basic fabrics. The sartorial drama between the sexes became more acute than it had ever been.

Along with modern English woolen tailoring for men's coats, modern long trousers came into existence as another example of startling and subversive male fashion. They chiefly derived from the French Revolutionary working-man's *sans-culotte* costume, although they were also worn by British common sailors and colonial slave-laborers, and had been occasionally used by gentlemen both for active sportswear and for leisure in those same colonies. But apart from their exciting plebeian connotations, they created an undemanding loose alternative to the close-fitting silk knee-breeches and skin-tight doeskin pantaloons of the late eighteenth century—clothes which had shown off the male legs and crotch without much room for compromise.

Trousers did not require a perfect body, and they had a nicely daring, casual look in themselves. They were instantly modified from their working-class simplicity and assimilated into the subtle tailoring scheme already developed for the elegant male coat of the new nineteenth century. The tube-like coverings for the legs answered harmoniously to the tube-like sleeves of the coat; and when the coat-skirts began consistently to veil the clearly delineated crotch of earlier days, the brilliantly colored necktie asserted itself, to add a needed phallic note to the basic ensemble.

The modern masculine image was thus virtually in place by 1820, and it has been only slightly modified since. The modern suit has provided so perfect a visualization of modern male pride that it has so far not needed replacement, and it has gradually provided the standard costume of civil leadership for the whole world. The masculine suit now suggests probity and restraint, prudence and detachment; but under these enlightened virtues also seethe its hunting, laboring, and revolutionary origins; and therefore the suit still remains sexually potent and more than a little menacing, its force by no means spent during all these many generations. Other ways for men to dress now share the scene with suits, so suits have shifted their posture; but they remain one true mirror of modern male self-esteem. Later we will follow their history and consider their fate more closely.

FEMALE INVENTION

BUT MEANWHILE, what about women? Did their clothes contribute anything important to the successive modernizations of dress, to the true development of fashion rather than its static variation? What fundamental new things have they worn without copying men? One thing to notice first might be whether men have ever copied women, and borrowed any compelling effects from specifically female trappings.

One feminizing male theme did appear in the Renaissance, in the décolleté necklines worn for a few years around 1500 by elegant young men, like Dürer in his self-portraits of 1493 and 1498, or by the male subjects of Titian's and Giorgione's portraits during the same period. The fashion gives a strong feminine cast even to images of bearded men, since an open neckline was already a basic feature of women's clothes. It also suggests a certain vulnerability that has little to do with standard male ideals of strength and ruthlessness or of austerity and aloofness. It has a marked passive erotic flavor, and was often doubtless intended to suggest the sexual as well as the sartorial modes of antiquity.

In the late Middle Ages women's necklines could be lowered because all clothes for both sexes began to be more close-fitting; an open neck would no longer make the dress fall off. One can see why men might also use the open neck for a time as an alluring device, to give their clothes a delicate flavor suitable for gentlemen engaged in contemplative or artistic pursuits, but also to show off fine neck muscles and handsome clavicles. Even among the tough Swiss mercenaries of the early sixteenth century the low open neckline appears as a good foil to exposed hairy legs, a big padded codpiece and vigorously slashed sleeves. But this vogue was very short-lived for men, a Humanist fashion connected with the revival of ancient learning and ancient bodily preoccupations, but unsuitable in succeeding generations devoted to religious strife and the spread of modern empire.

Although it has sometimes looked feminine to unaccustomed eyes, the long loose hair often worn by men was recurrently adopted (sometimes in wig form) as a feature of basic masculinity, Samson-style, not as a feminine touch. Loose, free hair was in fact rarely used by women without any elaboration or other head-dressing elements. The long hair of women was braided, knotted up, curled up, and interwoven with trimmings or covered: during the history of the West, only the Virgin and other virgins normally wore completely undressed long hair when fashionably dressed up.

Loose female hair was always a specifically sexual reference, the sign of female emotional looseness and sensual susceptibility, and a standard sexual invitation—Mary Magdalene wears it. This is still the case in current fashion, another sign of female reliance on ancient themes. Like female sexual desire, loose hair in the past was a potent female attribute not correctly displayed in public. But respectable unmarried girls, just like the Virgin Mary, wore loose hair to suggest the power of absolute female chastity. Their desire was unawakened like that of children, and their cloak of hair was a pure gift from God like the clothing of the field-lilies, a kind of edenic, surrogate nudity. Unawakened desire in a full-grown girl is moreover undissipated and unadulterated, full-strength and ready, a powerful asset. Queen Elizabeth I wore loose hair at her coronation, along with pounds of jewels and brocade, to advertise her virgin status as part of her power, both sexual and temporal. Brides also wore it. Virgin saints in pictures wear it. Respectable matrons might even have their portraits painted with their hair down, in a double feminine ploy suggesting both domestic chastity and erotic potency at the same time. For most women, it was necessary to *have* long thick hair, so as to be seen to have sexuality, but to show it publicly under very strict control.

By contrast, loose hair for mature men was usually a public virile ornament, akin to the display of muscle and stature, a sign of sexual force in action. It only looks feminine when it first becomes modish, after an extended short-haired period in male fashion. Then long hair gets the immediate disapproval of conservative observers who still associate it with female license. As is so often the case, what was an ancient sign of public strength in men was a sign of personal vulnerability in women; and some of that rubs off on men when they first adopt long hair—or indeed when fashion shifts the other way, and they begin to stop liking it. Some of the free-swinging loose hair of modern women can even count as another male borrowing in these enlightened times, just like their very, very short haircuts. It can now be one way to show pure sexual strength without admitting any mythological feminine weaknesses.

Clever décolletage, on the other hand, can be counted as a truly serious and thoroughly female contribution to fashion. It includes not only the neckline, front and back, but the line at which sleeves are cut to expose the wrist or any part of the arm and shoulder. Eventually the final modernization in this vein was the irreversible shortening of the skirt itself in this century, an act performed in several stages, just like the earlier ones exposing the upper body. In that vein, the latest modern female move has been the baring of the midriff—a new option, not a necessity.

Curiously enough, the most extreme shortening of skirts has seemed to bring women's clothing full circle once again, back into the sphere of men. The very, very short skirt appeared in the 1960's just at the time that pants became generally universal for women; and the miniskirt appeared belatedly to echo the scandalous exposure of male legs in the late Middle Ages—another male borrowing from the beginning of modernity in fashion. Girls acquired a page-boy look, with endless legs in bright tights descending below tiny little tunics.

Interesting exposure above the waist, however, was the most important female initiative in fashion for centuries; and male fashion has rarely imitated it, for neck or arms or midriff. Modern men's short-sleeved formal shirts, often forbidden in strictly correct circumstances, have their disturbing flavor partly because they were really borrowed from women, for whom arm exposure is respectable. Men have allowed themselves to take their shirts off, or to roll up the sleeves and unbutton the collar, in negligent or hearty modes; but they have not been moved to cut open the neckline or cut the sleeves so as to expose the skin in interesting ways. Nor did they ever do so with coats, gowns and doublets, all during fashion's long history. Even very short shorts for men, along with skin-exposing undershirts, both quite recently adopted, are also slightly disturbing as public male garments for city wear—I believe because they also have dared to borrow the modern female rule for ordinary exposure. In antiquity, of course, it went the other way: men were bare and women covered.

Skirts, those great traditional garments, also count as an original and purely female element, when they hang from the waist. Since their beginnings in the sixteenth century, they have never been borrowed for normal male dress. The kilt, the male garment that looks most like a skirt, is in fact a survival from the ancient days of general masculine drapery even for war. All the interesting female headgear developed from the veil into coifs and stiffened hoods of remarkable kinds was another female invention, and it was never imitated by men at all. If scholars and old men sometimes wore female-looking fitted caps to keep out the cold, they wore honorable male hats on top of them when they went out. Male hoods and cowls were either clerical, like gowns, or an unfashionable plebeian protection against weather. Now we see them on sweatshirts and parkas.

General progress in purely female modernization was slow. Although the neckline began exposing the chest quite early, the shortening of the sleeve was not accomplished until the seventeenth century, when the forearm was cautiously bared for the first time. Arms were eventually

LEFT: Anthony Van Dyck, *Henri II de Lorraine, duc de Guise,* 1634. BELOW: Anthony Van Dyck, *Henrietta Maria of France, Queen of England, with her Dwarf,* mid-1630's.

The duke's flowing hair, big feathery hat, big drooping collar and crumpled cloak and boots further relax a loose-fitting costume that no longer crisply models the body's separate parts. The painted terrain behind him adds still more wildness and asymmetry to the fashionably casual effect. Below, the queen now fingers the mobile folds of her skirt, instead of grasping a handkerchief. Her very low neckline has been topped off with a dashing masculine collar, and her hat and coiffure also echo the male mode; but her naked forearms are a new and purely feminine accessory. The painter has given them great prominence, along with the tactile pleasure her hands are feeling from the satin and the monkey's fur.

Jan Vermeer, *Man and Woman Drinking Wine,* Dutch, c. 1660.

This Dutch bourgeoise wears a conservative version of advanced feminine fashion, still not essentially altered since the Renaissance, with no male references and a modest stiffened veil covering her hair. The new, dropped shoulder-line of her dress ensures that her arms are held close to her body, even while it exposes more skin above; she has no mobile accessories. Her male companion, by contrast, may fling his great cape around him, stick out his elbows and flaunt his great white collar and cuffs, his great black hat.

exposed to the elbow, echoed by further exposure up above, as the neckline was hugely widened and bare shoulders rose up out of it. In fashion at that moment around 1660, the naked feminine wrist and soft forearm, so suggestive of more smooth softness inside the clothes, had finally made a clear link with the naked chest and shoulders; it was another electrifying and irreversible move.

The impulse continued toward extreme exposure for the whole upper body, accompanied by even more extreme upholstery and drapery for the lower half. The idea culminated in the fashionable evening dresses of the later nineteenth century, when the whole arm was exposed along with most of the chest, back and shoulders, and the sleeves of the evening dress became vestigial. The rib-cage and waistline were strictly compressed while the elaborate skirt took on ever more shape, scope and density.

The woman was thus even more emphatically divided into top and bottom. The fashion went to final extremes in the mid-twentieth-century revival, when the sleeve was wholly discarded and the strapless dress invented, with a tight chrysalis encasing the ribs and bust above a sweeping or clinging skirt, the arms now fully exposed to include not only naked back, chest and shoulders, but also naked armpits. The theme of nearly nude top and very shrouded bottom remains compelling in the present world, and it seems suitable for moments when the historical and romantic view of women has license to prevail—at the ball or the wedding, and often on the stage or screen.

It corresponds to one very tenacious myth about women, the same one that gave rise to the image of the mermaid, the perniciously divided female monster, a creature inherited by the gods only down to the girdle. Her voice and face, her bosom and hair, her neck and arms are all entrancing, offering only what is benign among the pleasures afforded by women, all that suggests the unreserved, tender and physically delicious love of mothers even while it seems to promise the rough strife of adult sex. The upper half of a woman offers both keen pleasure and a sort of illusion of sweet safety; but it is a trap. Below, under the foam, the swirling waves of lovely skirt, her hidden body repels, its shapeliness armed in scaly refusal, its oceanic interior stinking of uncleanness.

It is really no wonder that women seeking a definitive costume in which to enact their definitive escape from such mythology should choose trousers. Articulating female legs at last must have seemed—no doubt unconsciously, since the original arguments were all about convenience—a necessary move in the theater of sexual politics. Demonstrating women's full humanity was essential; and that meant showing that they had bodies not unlike men's in many particulars. To show that women have ordinary working legs, just like men (not exquisite machines for dancing and acrobatics, flashing under tinselly froth, nor seductive members like nether arms that entice only to clasp and strangle), was also to show that they have ordinary working muscles and tendons, as well as spleens and livers, lungs and stomachs, and, by extension, brains.

III. THE GENESIS OF THE SUIT

THE GREAT DIVIDE

MODERN SUITS really started in the later seventeenth century, when some sort of loose-fitting buttoned coat became the single most desirable upper garment for men. The modern suit-coat, in an early form, finally replaced both the gown and the padded doublet that had represented male elegance for three centuries. Below such a coat, elegant men still wore breeches with stockings, not trousers; but breeches stopped being laced to the doublet, lost all their padding, and became low-slung, loose and soft. A buttoned waistcoat appeared behind the opening of the coat, which was now left partly or altogether open as part of the desirable Baroque effect. The three-piece suit was born.

Soft shirt collars and cuffs replaced stiff ruffs; and for the first time some kind of cravat went around the neck. The coat-waistcoat-and-pants-with-shirt-and-tie scheme that I now loosely call a "suit" began the early stages of its long life. I want to propose that the defining element for modernity was not the use of one fabric—although that was certainly one meaning of "suit," and now the only one—but the abstract tripartite envelope with a unifying, loosely fitting shape, along with the shirt and tie. For two centuries, most coats were made in different fabrics from the pants, and still different from the waistcoat; if they were all the same, the costume was called "a suit of dittoes."

These early developments coincided with a new upper-class male desire to look rather easily clad, instead of meticulously trussed up and stowed away, as gentlemen in armor-like doublets had done for so long. They also gave the first suggestions, expressed in the casual style, of a changed military ideal and of the enduring conception that men's clothes are honest, comfortable and utilitarian, whereas women's are difficult, deceptive and foolish.

Both sexes were nevertheless wearing high heels at the time, often embellished with large rosettes; and as the seventeenth century went through its second half, the nearly universal male use of wigs kept men's clothes thoroughly committed to a show of artifice. Long hair had a temporary vogue for men during the first half of the century, as it had often done before and since; but the wigs designed to imitate it became deliberately fake and stayed that way for more than a hundred years. Suits may have started, but their easy look was overborne by the look of extreme contrivance on the head and feet.

The virile hair of Samson, stylized in wig form, moreover retained its quality of masculine privilege, as hats also still did—the phallic finishing touch, the separate male headpiece. Women rarely wore full wigs, but augmented their natural hair with all manner of false pieces, padding, wiring and eventually powder, without usurping the glorious false male crown. With all the new looseness in the shape and fit of male clothes, men's court suits continued to be made of rich and heavy fabrics, and shirts carried prodigious amounts of lace. Embroidery, ceremonial swords, and other showy adornments remained suitable for gentlemen until well into the eighteenth century. Elegant men had discovered a certain amount of physical mobility for the fit of their garments, but the idea of Nature and any true simplicity had to wait until much later.

On the other hand, a most prophetic "modern" thing about late-seventeenth-century suits was the esthetic distance they quickly travelled, during the decades between 1660 and 1690, away from any affinity with female costume. During the first half of the century, well-dressed men and women had had a fairly similar look, with loose curled hair, broad lace collars, and big hats on both sexes, and both in garments of mobile, shining silk with a similar kind of ornamentation and a similar bulkiness around the waist and hips—at the time, women's corsets were very shallow and gripped only the rib-cage. After 1660, the new, long and loose-fitting male coats began to appear in dark and even dull fabric; and soon all suit-coats had big flapped pockets and big cuffs, and many prominent rows of buttons appeared on pockets, cuffs, coat-front, and vest-front. Rows of braid, borrowed from ordinary soldiers and soon to be a standard military motif, were used for masculine trim even on rich court dress; hats and sword-belts were large and assertive to match the vast wigs. Boots were enormous, sculptural affairs with wide tops exposing separate linings.

During the same period, elegant women's costume, by contrast, went on to become much more stiffly and tightly fitted around the whole upper body, and began to be made of light-colored stuff that increasingly did a lot of episodic, decorative draping. Décolletage was more emphatic than ever, and women wore no buttons, flaps, cuffs, belts or pockets at all, nor any suggestions of loose fit or military braid. Hats were rare, but dainty lace headdresses came into vogue; and women's hair was their own, with some help. In the modest bourgeois vein, women's dress was sober and self-contained while men's was assertive and dashing, even in dim colors.

Such differences went along with a profound split that occurred in the craft of tailoring during the reign of Louis XIV, a split that had very lengthy effects. In 1675 a group of French seamstresses successfully applied for royal permission to form a guild of female tailors for the making of women's clothes—to become the first professional dressmakers. Louis approved, believing that the dignity of French women would be well served by such a development, which permitted scope for their talent, respect for their modesty, and independence for their taste. Increasingly thereafter, as all of Europe copied French fashion and fashion methods, women dressed women and men dressed men.

Although this was a change originally inaugurated by women for their own profit, it nevertheless worked to their ultimate disadvantage, as the whole of fashion was progressively divided into respectable tailoring for men and frivolous "Fashion" for women. "Fashion," as opposed to developments in tailoring, came to be something created and consumed by women, which consequently was seen to work, one way or another, to the disadvantage of the male sex and therefore to humanity as a whole.

The moment marked the beginning of a fundamental divergence in the clothes of the two sexes that affected the whole eighteenth century, reached an extreme in the nineteenth, and still persists. And from it also began the unique and remarkable development of the modern masculine suit with its distinctive abstract looks, which were so much at odds with all the women's clothes designed during the suit's long ascendancy.

Before this, after true fashion began in the late Middle Ages, we have seen that male tailors had made the clothes for both sexes, and that for four centuries a certain harmony was maintained between the separate kinds of sexual symbolism in dress. Clothes for men and women differed in shape, which made for different erotic emphasis, and men's fashion had always taken the imaginative lead; but male and female garments were nevertheless quite similar objects before the late seventeenth century. With all their differing suggestive components, they were nevertheless conceived and made on the same principles of craftsmanship, out of the same materials; and for centuries neither sex was more ornate than the other.

During all that time, men had designed, measured, cut out and fitted everybody's clothes, and other men had constructed them, with padding and boning and stuffing and stiffening to suit the mode for both sexes. Tailors' guilds had as much importance as other craft and professional institutions, and like them were wholly male. Clothing itself, now submitting to fashion, thus had an honorable place among established artisanal products. Professional seamstresses also existed; they were employed by tailors to do the necessary handwork on seams, trim and finishing. Shirts, underwear, household linen and children's clothes were also made by women, although often at home and not by professionals. Female plain sewing thus had altogether less honor than male tailoring.

Women were never tailors, trained to create design, cut, and fit— not master-tailors, nor journeyman-tailors, nor apprentices; but they were acknowledged experts at fine needlework. They not only did untold miles of necessary basic sewing both at home and for hire, but they traditionally excelled at lace-making, embroidery, and the fabrication of elaborate accessories. The idea seems to have been that women were both fanciful and diligent, and clever with their hands, but not essentially imaginative, that is, not *technologically* imaginative. After the foundation of the dressmakers' guild, and the spread of the idea that female dressmakers were appropriate for the making of women's clothes, male tailoring proceeded as before according to its craft tradition, but only for men, while dressmaking provided larger ornamental possibilities for women. A difference in the way clothes were conceived and made for the two sexes came into existence for the first time, a separation that profoundly affected both the character and the reputation of fashion for the next two centuries, and that still survives.

During the two hundred years before this split occurred, stays made of metal, wood or whalebone had been sewn directly into women's dresses to shape them according to the mode, and similar stays had been sewn directly into men's doublets and the skirts of their coats. Stays and stiffening also went into collars and sleeves and headgear for both sexes, to hold them up or out. But by 1700, corsets—meaning separate boned undergarments that shaped the figure—had come into existence for women only; and throughout the eighteenth century these continued to be designed, cut, fitted and constructed by men. Separate corset-making was considered a logical division of the male tailor's art, descended from the armorer's like tailoring itself.

This meant that the new craft of dressmaking, now carried on by women, actually consisted of simply applying the fabric, often in folds and with very little cutting, to fit onto an already shaped torso, allowing much of it to drape as a skirt, and then adding sleeves. For such a dress, imaginative cutting and construction were not required. Since it was not constructed of many pieces to fit the whole body, it could also be easily taken apart and the fabric used again differently. Very early eighteenth-century portraiture shows some of the effects of this situation; the subject's torso is clearly very rigidly corsetted, but the dress is draped, perhaps expressly for the portrait, almost haphazardly around its stiff shape.

Clearly the new dressmaker's craft mainly demanded clever arrangement, and true female elegance lay in the exquisite finish of surface details, the sort of thing women were traditionally good at anyway. The cut and fit that made the essential shape of the torso were devised by the male corset-maker; and although his handiwork did not seize the eye on the surface, where fashionable impact was created, the man-made corset was still the anchor for the whole composition until the nineteenth century. Corset-making was then taken over by women, too, often in factories; and women could become entirely responsible for the looks of female clothes from the skin out, except for shoes.

The elegance of men's clothing continued to depend, as always, on subtle but fundamental alterations of cut, which meant overall changes of shape, with trim adjusted to match. These could count as basic innovations in the progress of a serious craft, rather like architecture. By contrast, women's elegance was an affair of temporary effects, rather like festival decoration or stage design. Principles of actual design were not then applied to the cut of dresses, which continued to develop conservatively, the more so in the hands of dressmakers remote from the more dynamic tailoring tradition. In the eighteenth century, elegance for women was moreover not confined to the rather basic and limited efforts of dressmakers, but created by the enormously expensive *modistes* or *marchandes de modes*, women who specialized in making and arranging the ephemeral trim and small accessories that gave feminine fashion its increasingly bad reputation for frivolity and extravagant costliness.

Although such a division between the sexes might seem like a first advance into imaginative freedom for women, and a first retreat into the bondage of dull convention for men, the psychological and social results were the opposite, over the course of the eighteenth and nineteenth centuries. Male clothing, and by extension male regard for personal appearance altogether, continued to receive a respect proportionate to the respect given to all serious male enterprise, both technical and creative. The making of men's clothes was in fact a serious matter, involving the calibration and adjustment of the carefully designed paper pattern-pieces needed for the suit, and a refined skill, both in the cutting that translated them into fabric, and in the construction of the inner layers that created the hang of the garments. Above all, skill was required in the fitting to the individual figure without benefit of controlling undergarments. All this has still not changed in the custom tailor's craft, which is still carried on by men, as always with some women's help for the finishing processes.

But "Fashion" was gradually perceived anew, and soon appeared to be largely the unserious province of the women who created and consumed it. Since feminine fashion more and more consisted of ephemeral effects that changed very rapidly and noticeably, there was something in the idea, although nobody despised women's fine achievements in embroidery and lace-making, whichever sex they were made for. By the nineteenth century, however, men who concerned themselves less with the basic fit and suitability of their garments and more with its surface effect could be despised as effeminate, although such an association would never have been made about Henry VIII or any other gentleman in Renaissance days. It was also not yet automatically made in the last half of the seventeenth century; the diaries of Samuel Pepys and John Evelyn are full of uninhibited personal interest in the details of masculine fashion. But by 1714, Shaftesbury was already saying that serious art was compromised by too much interest in surface decoration. This is not so revolutionary a view; but he also said that a whole society with more taste for decorative than for serious art could rightly be called "effeminate."

Exempt from the evolutionary laws that govern changes in a traditional craft, women could freely deploy their skill in surface fantasy. But they sacrificed the claim to importance that is always made by any effort to innovate within the strict boundaries imposed by a powerful technical tradition. Stylistic change in any practical craft is rarely sudden, since prevailing technical means and materials tend to temper mercurial changes of taste, and customary procedure acts as a brake on unbridled fancy. Meanwhile any sort of invention that makes new and original use of standard practice without rejecting it is rightly seen to be seriously creative, the inspired answer to a difficult challenge.

If the shape of the complete costume is the medium, restraint must be exercised simply to keep the clothed body socially intelligible and not ridiculous. The skilled tailor follows the customer's wishes; but he must translate any wild vagaries the client may propose into serviceable arti facts. To do this, he can make a real change in established methods, but the modification must still stay in harmony with normal custom, so the client does not look a fool and his tailor an incompetent. None of this constrained the modiste, who had special license to add startling or outrageous productions on top of the dressmaker's simple shape, which consequently needed to change very little.

The inspired masculine tailor might also have his own bold ideas, but he would carefully adjust them to prevailing taste for clients who wished to try something interesting but didn't want to look daring. Thus the craft of tailoring developed its technical history slowly, and its artisans gradually learned new practices without having to throw out old

OPPOSITE TOP: Jean de St.-Jean, *Habit d'épée,* French fashion print, 1685. OPPOSITE BOTTOM: Nicolas Bonnart, *Anne de France, Daughter of Louis XIV,* French fashion print, c. 1695. LEFT: Jean de St.-Jean, *A Lady Walking in the Country,* French fashion print, c. 1680.

The modern suit-coat makes its first appearance, along with the necktie; but shapely legs are still a male fashionable necessity, and so is a mane of flowing hair, now worn in wig form. In aristocratic life, feathers, ribbons and lace deck men and women equally, and high-heeled shoes are worn by both; but (opposite bottom) only for riding would a lady wear a male coat and hat, neckwear and big wig. Otherwise (left) she would retain the low neck and veiled hair of feminine custom, even though her curls might elegantly escape. Her dress is fitted onto the hidden corset and draped at sleeve and skirt, which here shows its traditional double character very clearly.

hard-won skills or any fundamental understanding of the craft. If new materials became available, they were first adapted to old methods, which in turn were adapted to encompass them.

Modern technical inventions, like the sewing machine, have tended to be used at first to create things that looked made in the old way. Synthetic fabrics were first used to imitate natural ones; only slowly does new technology affect style as a whole. In the astonishing history of modern men's tailoring, this effect has been quite obvious. Inexpensive mass-produced suits are now made with varying kinds of fused synthetic materials for the invisible interlinings that shape the garment; but the desired effect remains that of hand-tailoring and hand-finishing, just as it was two hundred years ago. Outside where it shows, synthetic fabrics are either blended with natural ones to preserve the look of nature, or to mimic it carefully.

REASON AND FANTASY

BY THE SECOND HALF of the eighteenth century, feminine dress had acquired a fast-moving theatrical style of presentation increasingly given up by male tailors, who went on basing their own constant changes on evolutionary principles. Since these tended to involve the whole costume at once, the effects were fairly subtle. Vigorously noticeable fashion was feminine, gradually becoming more preposterous and wayward, apparently allied with all that could be thought deliciously undisciplined about women in general. Mainstream masculine fashion, though equally mobile, was generally less spectacular from mid-century on, and has consistently received much less popular attention, although it has enjoyed much more honor.

The increasing separation in the way the sexes wished to appear is manifest in the portraits of couples during the 1770's and 1780's, both English and European, and in the popular prints and fashion plates showing a male and female figure together. Men's suits, although they still might be made of embroidered silk and worn with wigs and lace-trimmed shirts, were shown much reduced in overall bulk, whereas women's attire had prodigiously expanded. Back in 1700, men had still kept to the Baroque ideal of innovative male expressiveness in dress, the big wig included, and women still looked stiffer, more restrained, and smaller in scope; but by 1775, the refining skills of male tailors and the fanciful efforts of the feminine modistes were showing their deep differences.

In all the pictures, the woman takes up twice as much room as the man. In the French fashion plates, the feminine figure is filled out with puffy fichus, ballooning skirts covered with bubbly furbelows, vast air-borne hats festooned with ruffles and garlands, supported by mountains of frizzed and fluffed hair. The whole cloud-like ensemble is further attended by the movement of thin veils and ribbons that catch the air as the lady walks.

The man may be nearly a foot shorter. His body forms a slender unit, his wig displays its tight curls with restraint, and his neat hat is of a modest size. His silken legs and arms are so free of extra fabric that they even look spindly, and his narrow shoulders carry no distracting ribbons or draperies. His waistcoated stomach curves smoothly out between his open coat-fronts, balancing the gentle flare of the coat-skirts astern. He looks a little like the lady's page or child—unless you wish to see him as her guide or keeper, a responsible man with a large decorated beast on a leash or a full-rigged ship in tow. The strong differences in the dress of men and women that appeared in the art of 1400 had none of this sort of imbalance.

Later eighteenth-century male tailoring seems to have followed a general movement of material taste away from Baroque eloquence to-ward greater simplicity and less breadth of display. Male tailors for women might have done the same for women's clothes; and indeed male tailors always did make the riding clothes worn by fashionable women, which were designed and made according to masculine models but with a skirt instead of pants. Since the late seventeenth century, such riding gear represented a constant female effort to share in masculine traditions, at least among the upper classes, including a share in the sexually neutral activity of riding to hounds. Serious riding clothes might have a more sober flavor than the other provocative masculine effects used by fast, fashionable women; but they might also be very erotic themselves, fitting tightly over corsets as they were made to do, and always indicating that supposedly male forms of sexual fantasy might be at work in the female imagination.

But for the drawing-room and the ballroom, for the street and for church, feminine modistes took the idea of refinement straight into the domain of feminine fantasy almost in a literary style, seeming to imitate sentimentality, pietism, "Gothick" preoccupations, the cult of feeling, and other aspects of eighteenth-century culture not visible in the advance of the masculine mode. Only women could wear full-rigged ships and model villages on their heads in 1778. By this period, expressing visual fantasy *in dress* was an entirely female privilege. Gentlemen now deliberately held aloof from allowing their clothed bodies to be elaborate works of visual art, as Henry VIII's had been, fully as much as Elizabeth I's, or as Charles I's had been, fully as much as Christina of Sweden's. Men's fanciful productions became detached from their physical selves— and apparently, women became detached from men.

The physical sexual identities of men and women have recently been described by Thomas Laqueur in "Making Sex" as having been reconstructed during the seventeenth century; and later shifts in the character of male and female sartorial expression seem to bear him out. What he calls a "two-sex model" of sexual identity gradually came into existence, whereby men and women were perceived to belong to wholly separate and distinct sexes, "opposite" in the modern phrase. This model replaced a much older view of them as correspondingly arranged versions of the same single human sex, with Woman at a less fully realized stage than Man. The difference was then measured by a single standard, which endowed women with less of the essential heat that thrust men's genital organs outward, and gave men an active imagination as well as an active will and judgment, the desire to create and consider ideas, objects or situations external to themselves. Woman's deficient force kept both her imaginative and procreative machinery within the compass of her body, where her reproductive organs were exactly like Man's, only constructed in reverse.

The later idea of Woman, which freed her from the appearance of being simply an un-expressed Man, gave women a whole separate

LEFT: *Marie Antoinette and Louis XVI,* French fashion print, c. 1778. BELOW: Jacques-Louis David, *Portrait of A. L. Lavoisier and His Wife,* 1788.

Male fashion contracts while the female version expands. Fantasy and excess are now the proper fashionable attributes of feminine dress only, while male elegance is increasingly restrained. The queen is covered with embellishments and her hair and dress, like those of the scientist's wife, help increase her overall size. The king keeps his embroidered waistcoat, but his suit is plain and his wig small, while the scientist is in unworldly black; and each still carefully shows a well-turned leg. Print-maker and painter have both composed pictures that emphasize feminine billow in the ascendant and masculine compression somewhat in retreat.

"sphere" in which to take imaginative exercise; but with all its foundations in somewhat more advanced knowledge of anatomy and a new idea of causality, its approved limits also seem to have kept female minds firmly linked to female bodies, and much more firmly linked than ever before to the task of embodying male fantasies. The imaginative gifts of women could apparently be best employed in creating themselves according to masculine visions—to build, as it were, a perpetual superstructure on the controlling shape of the corset, which was hidden from Man's eyes, so he could forget he had originally made it.

The startling changes wrought in the clothed appearance of the two sexes between, roughly, 1675 and 1775 look very much like a figurative illustration of the perceptual shift that Laqueur describes. Women's sexuality, as expressed in clothing increasingly created by women for themselves, moved quickly away from appearing as a more conservative and passive version of vigorous male expression, with occasional piquant borrowings from male usage, and toward a quite separate set of self-perpetuating fashionable references. These more and more described collective feminine imagery directly through the constant reshaping and rearranging only of conventionally feminine accouterments—beguiling headgear, décolletage, and the ancient feminine skirt. These took on more independent life.

As female fashion became more autonomous, women's skirts spread out into variable shapes less related to male coat-skirts; and women's hats, shoes and gloves for the first time became quite different from men's. Women began to create even more evocative pictures out of their own physical selves; men continued safely relying on the externally established tailoring tradition for the creation of an acceptable body, while they allowed their fantasies to appear in works of fiction and art, or indeed in science, politics and philosophy. Their fantasies about women were now interpreted freely by women themselves in the realm of feminine fashion, where Otherness had full scope.

IT IS TEMPTING to speculate about the possible results if all of women's fashion had continued to be men's direct responsibility during the course of the eighteenth century, instead of just corsets and riding habits. Despite strong social forces separating the sexes in other ways, and gradually marginalizing female effort, female dress might still have echoed the increasingly restrained masculine program in sartorial expression, following after men as it had formerly done. The final modernization of women's dress might even have occurred a century earlier than it did, at the same time as men's. The whole enterprise of "Fashion" might have avoided some of its later reputation as the outward sign of distinctively female superficiality and moral weakness, instead of being seen as a human imaginative effort just like any other, which may be overdone or underdone by bunglers of either sex, just as it may be well done by both.

But since the clothes of the two sexes together may always be seen as the image of a relation, it's clear that by the end of the eighteenth century, the look of male tailoring had become not just simpler, according to the fashion in all material taste, but even more aggressively simple as feminine modes became more fanciful. The advance of restraint as a quality of male dress may well have been hastened, spurred by the extremity of ladies' fashionable excesses, of which the folly could only be something sane men should be clearly seen to avoid, even if they liked it on the ladies.

Exceptions to these generalizations instantly present themselves—Robespierre, for example. The most famous portrait of this grim architect of the Terror shows him clad in varieties of brightly striped silk; and his costume for the 1794 Festival of the Supreme Being shortly before his execution was described as made of vivid blue and white silk, with a wide silk tricolor sash, a plumed hat and a bouquet as an accessory. He, Saint-Just, and certain other fierce members of the French Revolutionary government seem to have dressed with a colorful exuberance then seen mainly on women, and with the sort of richness seen mainly on nobles in earlier days, whatever their sex. A few French fashion plates of the moment show this bright male plumage, all of it tight-fitting and pared down in shape, just when the newest note of male chic in Paris was being struck by drab street-fashions that ran to loose laborers' pants and big ragged neck-cloths.

In England, a slightly earlier (late 1770's) flare-up of old-fashioned fantasy among gentlemen resulted in the style dubbed "Macaroni," which ran to huge wigs and tiny hats, vast buttons and killingly bright stripes. Very few wore the fashion and it didn't last or have an influence, but it got a lot of attention at the time and was of course scathingly called effeminate. Such brief but bright manifestations, in a general climate of increasing male simplicity, look from a distance like a trace of envy for the new female latitude in fashionable display. Powerful men were on the verge of having to give up all that for good, leaving it to vain women, actors, fools, and children.

Late in the nineteenth century and early in this one, men again commonly became designers of women's clothes. After the initial shock, female fashion began to regain some of the respect, equal to that for men's tailoring, that it had once enjoyed during the Renaissance, when men were in charge of both. In fact the high standards of male tailoring came once more to be quite generally applied to elegant women's dress during the nineteenth century's last quarter, carrying on from traditional riding dress to develop other sorts of "tailor-made" ensembles for urban feminine life. Crisp shapes for the body and neat headgear had a strong appeal in a period of social revolution and social reform, including the reform of women's lives and minds. At the same time, fantasy still reigned for ball-gowns and tea-gowns, and the elegant at-home costumes such as Proust describes.

Women, of course, eventually regained more respect altogether, which has attached to the work of female designers in this century as it has to that of female artists. The best modern work by women in fashion design has in fact gone straight in the opposite direction from surface froth, and concentrated intensely on serving the shape and movement of the complete female body itself. It has further insisted on conveying the wearer's overall physical awareness of her own clothing. This concentration did not seem possible for female dressmakers in earlier days, when women were dressing women chiefly for men to look at. Men evidently wished to see women as apparitions, not autonomous organisms. So long as that was true, women naturally took great pleasure in excelling at the apparition business, whether as makers or consumers of fashion.

SOBRIETY AND SIMPLICITY

APART FROM REACTION to the seventeenth-century dressmaker's revolution, there were other early forces at work on the genesis of the unassuming man's suit. A certain new desire for sober effects in men's fashion had arisen not only from the modish soldierly simplicity everywhere evident in the first half of the seventeenth century when all of Europe was at war, but by a new vogue for clerical modesty. Clerical dress acquired a strong visual presence in public life with the spread and power of Protestantism during the century; and the period also saw the rise of institutions founded on reason and empirical judgment. I am using "clerical" to refer to both religious and secular commitment to thought and learning, as well as to the honest practice and just administration of law.

For citizens of the rising merchant and professional classes, especially in Protestant countries, a dark and plain suit relieved by simple white linen reasserted its very old associations with clerical intelligence, further supported by suggestions of probity and religious integrity. At the same time, simple textures, including leather and plenty of buttons, obliquely suggested a potent, quasi-military readiness if not ruthlessness. Both of these effects first succeeded in the non-courtly bourgeois vein, in Northwest Europe and in England under the Commonwealth. Such a creative combination of opposites—the easy roughness of practical war gear blended with the reticence of clerical clothing—has had a lasting power over the masculine sartorial imagination.

War and religious fundamentalism both tend to dramatize the difference between the sexes. Even without the changes in tailoring practice inaugurated at the French court, the general scheme for dress in other countries in the later seventeenth century shows the sexual resonance of the religious wars that had gone on all over Europe for several generations after the Reformation, most comprehensively in the Thirty Years' War of 1618 to 1648. In the great Dutch paintings of the middle seventeenth century, for example, the difference between the stable beauty of the smooth-haired women in their shining heavy skirts and the easy swagger of the dull-coated men in their big hats and boots forms a large part of the modern appeal of these genre scenes. Men look simply and thickly dressed, and are mobile and relaxed; women look more carefully adorned, and are still and secret.

Such differences are absent from fifteenth- and sixteenth-century art, in the paintings of Piero della Francesca, or of Holbein, Breugel and Titian, where men and women of the same social rank wear different clothes, but are the same height, move the same way, and have the same degree of stability, flamboyance or shine. The new style of bourgeois sexual ambience apparent in the Dutch works and its corresponding fashionable ideals are congenial to the nineteenth- and twentieth-century ones increasingly founded on middle-class ideals. The changes brought about by Louis's 1675 agreement to let women dress themselves had their greatest appeal in a middle-class world that had its first broad effects in the eighteenth century, and increasing importance thereafter.

Male European court dress in the first half of the eighteenth century began to separate even further from crisp bourgeois modes and to look more cumbersome than imaginative. The feather-edged hats and be-ribboned braided coats worn at Versailles under Louis XIV, and continuing with modifications under the next two Louis, do not suggest the vitality of forward-leaping styles that plant seeds for the future. They held strictly to old views of dress that required richness of surface for high rank. Elegance in dress at court remained a matter of refinement in luxurious display, not of interesting changes in basic design.

The most vital forms of male elegance in the second half of the eighteenth century, in fact, were developed by the eccentric and unmodish male aristocracy of England, who increasingly scorned personal display and court ritual, while remaining somewhat aloof from the look of middle-class commercial success or of clerkly gravity. They adopted a sartorial blend of the chic plainness proposed by the Puritans of earlier days and by the country-dwelling yeomanry and gentry. To overtones of war and religion were thus added the potent flavors of leisured country life and country sport, which suggest the perennial conquest of brute nature.

This enterprise carries with it a certain sense of identification with both the hunted and the hunting beast; and English country dress, besides harmonizing with the earth and its fields, forests and rocks, came to suggest the comfortable coat of horse and dog, the smooth fit and dun color of the stag's hide. Wool and leather and linen came to give the gentleman's body a poetic harmony with his natural domain, rather than the look of opposition to it—a kind of dominion founded on love, not fear. Paintings by Stubbs of man and beast outdoors together show the desired effect at mid-century and after. Nature was generally coming into vogue during the later eighteenth century as a moral and esthetic influence far superior to all the vain and distorting efforts of civilization, and a mode of dress that seemed to embody it could not help but appeal.

The startling modernizations in male dress that occurred in England at the very end of the eighteenth century were thus already well prepared for, from the point of view of male distance from female modes, and of retreat from old ideas of stiff bulk and weighty richness as signs of superiority in men's clothing. England at the time was a very technologically advanced, rich and democratic nation; the English had already beheaded their absolute monarch in the previous century, before Louis XIV had even taken hold in France. In England, a plain coat, useful boots, plain hat and plain linen were becoming the signs of a gentleman possessed not only of many acres and full coffers, but of a sensible mind with an adult disdain for primitive institutions and their personal fripperies, however exquisite. Wigs were worn, but much reduced in size. Opulent court dress might be worn, but only at obligatory court appearances at home and abroad.

In England, elaborate and gaudy garments in general became associated not only with Popery but with specifically feminine sexuality, and with France and Italy in their character as centers of passion, sensuality and superstition as well as of decayed feudalism and diabolic Catholicism. Paris was consequently more and more seen as the capital of feminine and not masculine fashion, as women seemed more and more to become the conductors of feeling and the repositories of either frivolous or forbidden fantasy—besides being as always the guardians of traditional

ABOVE: George Stubbs, *Sir John Nelthorpe Out Shooting with His Dogs in Barton Fields, Lincolnshire,* English, 1776. RIGHT: Louis Léopold Boilly, *Portrait of Chénard as a "Sans-Culotte,"* French, 1792.

The country-dwelling English aristocrat begins to set the fashionable male tone from now on: unpretentious simplicity, unadorned materials, perfect fit. Sir John still wears eighteenth-century breeches with his boots; but his dull colors and round hat are prophetic. Right, the French Revolutionary image offered another potent new element to future fashion: the rough laborer's trousers, along with an air of physical strength combined with slightly untidy youthful idealism.

common views, sometimes called old wives' tales. London, on the other hand, was the center of truly advanced male costume. Even by the 1780's, Frenchmen were agreeing with this idea, and a fashion for the simplicities of English male tailoring was already launched in France before the Revolution. For city wear, the walking-sticks and umbrellas suitable for right-minded gentlemen going about town on foot, as they did in London, began to replace the dress swords European nobles had worn while rumbling in gilded carriages en route to *salons* and *levées*.

BUT DURING THIS early rise of new English ideas about the right look for gentlemen's clothes, certain fundamental things applied. All men's suit-coats during the later seventeenth century and most of the eighteenth had no collar, despite the strong presence of cuffs and pocket-flaps, and no shaping at all at the shoulder. The only sort of gentleman's coat that did have a collar was a garment of no elegance, the informal woolen "frock" worn by Englishmen at private leisure in the country; and coachmen wore coats with cape collars, for protection against rain and snow.

Art of all kinds shows that throughout the period from 1650 to 1780 men's shoulders ideally looked very narrow and sloping and their chests somewhat sunken, and that even on slim figures the stomach swelled out prominently between the open coat-fronts and above the low waist of the breeches. This dome-like shape for the mid-section was emphasized by the descending row of waistcoat buttons that marched down its center, echoed by the coat buttons and buttonholes on either side. Coat-skirts, often stiffened or wired, swung outward at hip-level, both sideways and behind. Under the coat, the breeches were full around the hips and then buckled in at the knee, and stockings and medium-heeled shoes finished the ensemble below that, if boots were not worn.

The entire effect tended to emphasize a man's hips, belly, and thighs, shrink his chest and shoulders, lengthen his torso and shorten his legs. Richly embroidered or plain, all male figures were thus rendered slightly squat and infantine, and what we would call feminine, with the curled wig adding to the impression. This is, of course, a modern perception. The big wig and the cut of men's clothing were so distinctively masculine at the time that no one saw any femininity whatsoever in the pear-like form that art and fashion suggested was a man's ideal shape. The form itself, I would insist, had its own accumulated authority and was certainly carried with grace by many. The shape of dressed women was a complete contrast to it, conventionally feminine in age-old ways, with the severe suppression of the mid-section, much décolletage, and many varieties of aggressive-defensive skirt. No one could confuse them.

BUT HOW DID the look of modern man in his modern tailoring emerge from all this wrinkled fabric laden with rows of buttons, and covering pear-shaped male bodies down to the knee? To re-form, to "modernize" the whole shape of the ideal man (not just to change the fabrics and accessories that clothed him) required an imaginative force more immediate than the uncertain work of technological and social change. Clothes had certainly begun to look different in keeping with the earlier change in belief about the sexes; but it was under the influence of a new radical shift in visual style that the collective eye for the figure was abruptly retrained. Ever since, in contrast to the early versions we have so far described, all modern suits have been cut to suggest a male body that tapers from broad shoulders and a muscular chest, has a flat stomach and small waist, lean flanks and long legs. Modern developments of the elegant coat, waistcoat, shirt and pants since 1800 required not only new materials, but a new anatomical foundation. The one offering itself at the time, then present on the esthetic scene with fresh power, was the heroic male nude of Classical antiquity.

ANTIQUE NATURAL NUDITY

WHEN THE NEO-CLASSIC artists and designers of the late eighteenth century sought to convey modern ideas in radically antique form, Classical antiquity was nothing new. Educated Europe had been mining its themes and subjects and visual tropes for centuries, and artists had applied antique elements to every current formal idiom. But after about

1750, partly under the influence of engravings made from the discoveries at Pompeii and Herculaneum, visual consciousness of the antique was raised anew. It matched emergent ideas of Nature and Reason, even of Liberty and Equality, that seemed best cast in the most august and even primitive mold, unmodified by later fashionable distortions. The artistic life of all Europe was progressively transformed so as to employ the orders of Classical architecture and the figures of Classical art as much as possible in their original forms.

This meant looking again at the already well-known examples, besides pondering the new ones. In England, the climax of the movement occurred with the arrival of the Elgin Marbles in London in 1806, when after generations of engraved and reconstructed antiquities the English public could see examples of incomparable Greek sculpture face to face. But the heroic masculine figures on the Parthenon frieze and other glorious fragments now gave the Laocoön and the Apollo Belvedere, which had been admired in the Vatican collections since the Renaissance, a new vitality as modern standards for male beauty, even while their quality as sculpture was soon seen to be inferior to the Pheidian masterpieces. The Apollo's pose can be clearly seen as the foundation for many standing male portraits of the later eighteenth century, well before tailoring was changed to emulate the Classical figure more closely.

For its use of antiquity as a source of basic form rather than of surface allusion, the Neo-classic esthetic revival can be called an early version of modern design. Nikolaus Pevsner called it modernism's "first chapter." The two artistic movements shared a desire for a new "realism" in art that would denote respect for fundamental structure rather than insisting on surface verisimilitude. In France, architectural innovation was promoted in Classical terms by Claude Nicolas Ledoux, who was one of the first to borrow from ancient buildings their simple relationships among solid forms rather than their decorative motifs. His Paris *barrières* of 1784 have an unadorned modern look in their antique sobriety. In England, Sir John Soane's imaginative simplifications based on Classical sources seem equally modern, and they also give the further impression of carrying on a native plainness that was already dominant in English architecture and design.

For the dressed figure, analogous simplifications were now imperative for both sexes. The fundamental structure of the body was rediscovered, but entirely in antique form. The system of clearly delineated limbs, heads and muscles, of harmonious stomachs and buttocks and breasts that was perfected in antique nude sculpture was adopted as the most authentic vision of the body, the real truth of natural anatomy, the Platonic form. Clothing, instead of ignoring much of the actual body, as it had been doing for so long, was going to have to indicate a new understanding of such rediscovered "natural" anatomical facts. As usual, clothing in art took the lead.

In France, Jacques-Louis David and others provided paintings showing magnificent examples of correct anatomical and vestimentary form for both sexes, chiefly in legendary circumstances. Female portraiture, with its special license for fantasy in tune with female fashion, also became more authentically classicized. Similarly, for costume on the French stage, the difference between the old and new methods of Classical allusion appeared in the difference between a stage nymph of 1765, wearing a leopard skin over a corset and a spangled hoopskirt, along with high heels and powdered hair crowned with a garland, and a stage nymph in 1795, wearing the same wreath and leopard skin with loose hair and apparently nothing else but two yards of muslin. Talma, the famous French Revolutionary actor, appeared as an ancient Roman in the soft short tunic and sandals of a David painting, instead of the big stiff skirts, high heels and towering wig worn by all theatrical Roman heroes for a hundred and fifty years.

But as usual, more things were possible in art than in life. Tailors and dressmakers, now launched on separate paths, faced the problem of classicizing the actual figure according to their separate capacities. Johann Joachim Winckelmann, the great historian and exponent of Greek art, had urged that the modern artist must not simply copy the works of antique art, but must imitate the way the antique artist worked. Like Ledoux and Soane, the true Neo-classic artist should, as Panofsky interprets Winckelmann, "undergo a creative assimilation of his methods and not put together a scientific reconstruction of his results." In the realm of Neo-classic fashion, it was the male tailors of England who managed the first, just like the architects, and the feminine dressmakers of France who stayed with the latter, just like the costume designers.

One important ancient Greek convention had rendered the male figure in the nude, and draped the female body completely. Until late in the third century B.C., women in ancient Greek sculpture showed their beauties through a veil of delicate folds, while the hero wore nothing but his perfect nudity, perhaps enhanced by a short cape falling behind him. The nude costume was the one most suggestive of perfect male strength, perfect virtue and perfect honesty, with overtones of independence and rationality. The hero's harmonious nude beauty was the visible expression of his uncorrupted moral and mental qualities. Modesty, on the other hand, was already the signal female moral virtue; female zeal, energy or wisdom, or indeed sexual attractiveness, had to be filtered entirely through it, so to speak. The resulting combination could be nicely denoted by an enveloping garment that had a tendency to cling.

Dressmakers, already accustomed to creating theatrical styles of chic without much concern for cut, simply rearranged their materials to approximate the antique statues—the look of nudity, more or less thinly covered with drapery. Under the drapery would actually go flesh-colored body tights of varying kinds and new constructions for rounding and separating the breasts, all to create a new sort of theatrical effect. But tailors, still meeting the basic challenge to construct a complete three-dimensional casing for the male body, set out to re-create the antique nude hero entirely in terms of existing men's clothes.

Whereas late-eighteenth-century dressmakers and modistes were free to throw out the big hats and the ballooning hoops, and dress women in straight-falling muslin, the tailors were still bound by craft principles, and could not throw them out; they certainly could neither crudely denude the man nor put him in a stagey tunic. To convey the image of unadorned masculine perfection, they had to remodel the nude male wholly out of cloth, to create an abstract statue of the naked hero carved according to tailor's rules. This meant modifying the existing suit without giving up its basic components or departing from its methods of construction, and without exposing any skin at all.

Since the nude Classical figure had become the new image of natural man, a modern man might reasonably want a heroic figure without seeming to yearn foolishly for an impossible ideal. He would simply be expressing a wholesome wish for something normal, and now the tailor could arrange it. Fashionable tailors used ordinary clothes themselves to transform artificial, bewigged and Rococo man into noble and antique natural man. They offered the perfect Classical body, aptly translated into the modern garments that were the most traditionally "natural" in themselves, the ones that even further suggested the unfallen Adam in the Garden, the simple clothes of English country life.

But in the 1770's, these clothes still looked even more bunchy than elegant dress, which had been reduced in scope and sharpened up so much on both sides of the Channel. The loose and comfortable woolen frock with its turned-over collar might form the basic element for the new mode, but it needed serious revision. Big cuffs and pocket-flaps had to disappear. During the next twenty years, full coat-skirts shrank drastically and lost all their thickening and stiffening, which was instead transferred upwards to expand the chest and shoulders. Sleeves even acquired a small puff at the top to suggest firm deltoids. The waistcoat, formerly stretching well down over the rounded belly, was shortened and cut straight across at a high, neat waistline. Like the coat, it was often made double-breasted, to help suppress the old domed stomach with its long central row of buttons. The formerly floppy collar rose up to balance the enlarged shoulders, to strengthen the heroic neck and support the unpowdered head, now shorn of its wig and cropped in the Classical style.

Legs were clad from the high waist down to the ankle in one pale color, so they might sweep up in a flowing classic line instead of dividing at knee and groin with much horizontal bunching of the fabric. The very leggy nude art of the period was matched in actual dress by "pantaloons" of knitted silk or smooth doeskin, which gave the male figure a new genital emphasis that had been missing ever since the abandonment of the codpiece in the High Renaissance. However a man was really built, his tailor replaced his old short-legged pear-shaped body with a lean, well-muscled and very sexy body with long legs.

The new fashion was, however, undeniably hard on the truly fat. Caricatures appeared showing the humpty-dumpty effect of the high waist and minimal coat-tails on men with unquenchably big bellies, and those with spindly legs had to use calf-stuffers and thigh-improvers to produce the Classical norm. The loose fashions of former days had been much kinder to the bulky figure with skinny extremities; but quick developments in modern tailoring soon addressed the problem, so that suits could soon naturalize everyone. A more encompassing shape for the coat, combined with the use of trousers for elegant wear, later adjusted the scheme even more accurately to its nude Classical counterpart.

HEROES IN WOOL

BY 1810, the new tailoring techniques had already produced an unornamented sculptured coat, a loose envelope for the male upper body, subtly cut of dull material and sewn with highly visible seams. The essential texture and construction, not the surface richness, created its esthetic interest. This was a very modern idea; and it was possible only in an ancient tailoring tradition founded on the use of wool. English tailors had long been superior to all others in the cut and fit of woolen garments; and wool was known to be the great staple fabric of England since the earliest period of its history.

Wool was also known to be the common fabric of antiquity, and it was a satisfying fact that not only country coats but heroic togas were properly made of woolen cloth. Consequently for the creation of a natural man who was both modern and antique, the appropriate fabric was at hand in England, accompanied by materials of equal antiquity and simplicity such as smooth linen and varieties of leather, and colonial contributions such as cotton. Emergent national pride, expressing distance from French and other Continental influences, supported a fashion based mainly on native materials and native skills.

The English had certainly used silk, too; but the firm silk fabrics used for men's clothes had a taut and rigid weave, whereas all wool is flexible and elastic. Under the influence of steam, pressure and careful manipulation, to say nothing of imaginative cutting, wool can be made to stretch, shrink and curve at the tailor's will, to follow and complement the shapes and movements of the wearer's body without buckling and rippling. It truly resembles a sculptural medium, obedient to a designer's creative desire. Silk, on the other hand, asserts its own authority. The more simply cut silk and velvet coats of former days, suitable for the Rococo temper, had wrinkled with every movement of the wearer and with every bit of pressure on the buttons, partly because the fabric refused to stretch at all.

Works of art show that all those rows of buttons and buttonholes, those extra cuffs and flaps and applied embroideries, and all those long waistcoats, full skirts and soft breeches had created a network of little wrinkles over the whole body of the man. This engendered a surface motion that caught the light and made a further embellishment for the suit in wear. The body was always veiled by the rippling surface of its garments, which displayed the elegance of the wearer every time he drew breath.

But by the turn of the century, elegance had shifted entirely away from wrought surfaces to fundamental form, and away from courtly refinement to natural simplicity. And so tailors elevated the unfitted rough country coat into a triumph of art, whereby crude natural man became noble natural man, with references to ancient sculpture built into the structure of his clothes. With the help of nearly imperceptible padding, curved seams, discreet darts and steam pressing, the rough coat of dull cloth was gradually refined into an exquisitely balanced garment that fitted smoothly without wrinkles and buttoned without strain, to clothe what appeared to be the torso of a Greek athlete.

Its collar was forced by clever cut, steaming and stiffening to curve up and around the neck, to fold over and open out in front, and to form lapels that would obediently lie down and align themselves smoothly with the body of the coat. This perfectly tailored collar and flat-lying lapel still forms the most distinctive element of the modern suit-coat, and became the formal sign of modernity in dress. It is now so universal for both sexes that it is almost invisible. The art with which it is accomplished is also invisible, and the lapels of modern jackets look as if they lay flat by natural inclination.

The subtle lines of the coat formed an abstract design based on the underlying curves of human bone and muscle, and the matte texture suggested the smoothness of skin. The careful modelling allowed the actual body to assert itself only at certain places when the wearer moved, to create a vital interaction between costume and person, a nonchalant counterpoint again with echoes of an animal easy in its own skin. The discreet padding in the upper chest and shoulders was carefully thinned out over the chest and back and disappeared in the lower half of the coat, so that the effect was of a wholly unpadded garment, an apparently natural covering.

To go with this apotheosis of rough gear, the plain linen shirt and cravat, which might have been worn soiled and sloppily knotted by rough-living country gentlemen, were laundered into incandescent whiteness, lightly starched, and then folded with a sculptor's care around the neck and jaw, to produce a commanding set of the head on the heroic shoulders. The thick and muddy country boots were refined, fitted and polished to perfection, and the whole ensemble was ready for transfer from the hedgerows to Pall Mall. Adding spice to this potent mixture was the exciting urban contribution from across the Channel, the *sans-culotte* costume of the Revolutionary laboring classes. This similar Neo-classic "natural" mode could eventually be blended with the English version, refined and translated from the barricades to the drawing-room, bringing the spirit of revolt and suggestions of plebeian effort to the already powerful combination of ideas embodied in the new masculine costume.

Thus the male figure was recut and the ideal man recast. Formerly the play of light on rich and glinting textures had seemed to endow the gentleman with the play of aristocratic sensibility, and made him an appropriate vessel for exquisite courtesy, schooled wit and refined arrogance without having to reveal the true fiber and caliber of his individual soul any more than that of his body. Now the noble proportions of his manly form, created only by the rigorous use of natural materials, seemed to give him an individual moral strength founded on natural virtue, an integrity that flowers in esthetic purity without artifice, and made him a proper vessel for forthright modern opinion and natural candid feeling.

His garments made him look honest, since the seams showed and the weave was apparent in the plain fabric—and rational, because of the perfect cut, fit and proportions, which also gave him his artless good looks. The whole achievement had been accomplished entirely by simply reworking the old seventeenth-century scheme of coat, waistcoat, and breeches, with a shirt and some kind of cravat. It replaced the same scheme made of nude muscles that had been the Classical expression of the same virtues, and now gave the impression that the nude hero was even more natural when dressed.

All these new phenomena are associated with the legendary figure of Beau Brummell, who himself embodied the new kind of hero made by tailoring. In the new urban Dandy mode, a man's heroism consisted only in being thoroughly himself; Brummell proved that the essential superior being was no longer a hereditary nobleman. His excellence was entirely personal, unsupported by armorial bearings, ancestral halls, vast lands, or even a fixed address, and he was also known to be able to live on nothing a year. His garments had to be perfect only in their own sartorial integrity, that is, in form alone, unburdened by any surface indices of the worth attached to rank. Brummell himself was known to have wished his clothes to be unnoticeable.

Brocade and embroidery had once indicated the generic superiority even of quite inferior individuals, and had displayed the beauty of the costume, not the man. Careful fit without adornments, on the other hand, emphasizes the unique grace of the individual body—indeed creates it, in the highest tailoring tradition. The man's rank or even his deeds are irrelevant to the fine cut of his plain coat; only his personal qualities are shown to matter. Thus the Neo-classic costume was a leveller in its time, and has since remained one in its subsequent revisions, creating superior beings of all classes. The perfect man, as conceived by English tailors, was part English country gentleman, part innocent natural Adam, and part naked Apollo the creator and destroyer—a combination with an enduring appeal, in other countries and other centuries. Dressed form was now an abstraction of nude form, a new ideal naked man expressed not in bronze or marble but in natural wool, linen, and leather, wearing an easy skin as perfect as the silky pelt of the ideal hound or horse, lion or panther.

Not only the bodily proportions but the ideal color of the antique was sustained in the newly heroized country costume. In England and Northern Europe, all eighteenth-century Neo-classic art consistently emphasized a lucid monochromy. Suppressing the play of color led to a better appreciation of fundamental outline and form, and newly admired antiquities were most often reproduced in graphic outlines, the better to celebrate the simple purity of their shapes without irrelevant sensuous distractions.

The originally painted ancient marbles had become colorless by the time they were found, like the ancient buildings. The virtue of their colorlessness had been further supported by Michelangelo and the later sculptors who set out to rival antiquity in white marble. In those days such monochromy was usually offset by chromatic richness in all other modes of art and decoration, and classicizing Renaissance and Baroque painters had continued to use color and texture when rendering the antique in pictures. David and other French Neo-classic painters were also continuing to evoke the ancient world using the whole spectrum.

But the esthetic power of antique colorlessness was more thoroughly credited at the end of the eighteenth century than it had ever been before. In England, Holland, Scandinavia, and Germany, rich color lost its authority for a time—perhaps in part because of its associations with France, now replacing traditional royal license with tyrannical imperial pomp, after a fearful and bloody interval. The abandonment of color may have expressed the desire for a certain distance from these vivid developments; and it also seemed to support the idea of the search for Classical authenticity as a kind of purification, in alignment with Protestant impulses.

Sir Joshua Reynolds had written that lavish color in painting made a base appeal to sensuality, and that the play of light over rich texture had similarly vulgar attractions unworthy of the Great Style in painting, exemplified by Michelangelo. The Sistine Chapel frescoes were already faded and grayish in the eighteenth century; and they were admired all the more for their chromatic dullness, which suggested a much nobler vision of serious ancient events than anything devised in the shimmering styles of Titian or Rubens. Or in the current ones of David and Gérard, at work across the Channel.

Following the prevailing view expressed by Sir Joshua, the Neo-classic English tailors exploited the new prestige of muted color and matte finish. In clothing, these no longer conveyed sober humility but suggested the same Classical virtues that antique nudity itself embodied, including superior beauty. The new graphic rhetoric for ideal male looks forced the masculine costume not only to classicize its outlines but to lose much of its color and reflect no light—and to appear more beautiful as a result, not less so.

For men's clothes, clearly defined areas of black, brown, buff and white replaced the spread of fluid and shining colored stuffs. For coats, dark green and dark blue wool, suggestive of the natural world and the

RIGHT: Johann Joachim Winck-
elmann, drawing of a painted
Greek vase, from *Monumenti
Antichi Inediti*, 1767. BELOW:
Jacques-Louis David, *Madame
Récamier*, French, 1799.

LEFT: Thomas Hope, drawing of Jupiter, copied from a Roman monument, from *Costume of the Ancients,* English, 1812. LEFT BOTTOM: Fashion plate, *Grand Négligé,* from *La Mésangère,* French, 1808.

The ancient Greek vase shows a couple in characteristic costume—he is nude, she is thinly draped. The David portrait shows a fashionable adaptation: the dress is actually close-fitting around the upper torso, and the skirt carries most of its fullness high up at the back, to ensure a long, graceful sweep in wear. Her bare feet, bare surroundings and absence of jewels are all pictorial devices supporting the fantasy of classic simplicity. The drawing by Hope gives the correct Classical proportions for men: muscular chest and shoulders, lean flanks, long legs. These are all nicely echoed in the male fashion plate, which shows how the new simple tailoring creates a classic nude figure made entirely of wool, leather and linen. Jove now carries a swagger stick instead of a thunderbolt.

J. G. Bourdet, *Une Promenade,* French fashion print, 1838.

The brief classic moment is over for women; froth and bulk have quickly re-asserted themselves, but this time in Romantic terms. She is small and delicate, he is tall and masterful, still sexily wearing the costume of nudity translated into tailoring. Her long hair is well controlled and firmly covered, his is short, thick and free under a removable hat.

simple country life, might be included in the scheme. But a dull finish and clarity of line were essential. In accordance with the Neo-classic formula for rendering nature truly, a perfect linear composition was a more truthful and a more beautiful, and thus a *better* achievement than any worked-up, lustrous and multicolored finish, for artists and tailors both.

In the second act of modernism, during the first quarter of this century, a new radical view of the beauty of form was again accompanied by a certain retreat from color. The most extreme visions of Cubism tended to eliminate vivid hues in their concentration on the multiple truth of form. In architecture a new respect for the intrinsic beauty of naked steel, glass and concrete helped to revive a taste for formal value uncluttered by busy adornment, including the distracting beauty of color; and this taste was further supported by masterpieces of black and white photography and cinematography that celebrated only shape, line and surface texture. All this helped to keep the new versions of the modern masculine suit, now celebrating formal abstraction in new ways, on the same path toward muted color that they had originally taken during their first Neo-classic appearance.

NEO-CLASSIC EROTICS

THE CLASSICAL FOUNDATION for modern male tailoring has had another long-lasting effect. Just like ancient nude statues, men gradually came to look similar; and to desire to look similar. The greater uniformity among clothed men that characterizes the last two centuries, by comparison with the variety among women, was inaugurated at this same epoch. It was then another attribute of antique and natural virtue, representing the brotherhood of moral clarity and evenness of temper, and yet paradoxically offering a way to focus on the individual. Right now at the end of this century when world leaders come together, all wear similar suits that display the uniform desire for international harmony, even while each face appears all the more distinctive, clearly aware of separate responsibility. The individual tailoring for each suit also shows the flexible possibilities of a single scheme when faced with very different bodies, and the varieties of the same style desired by men of different cultures.

It had first become clear in the early part of the nineteenth century that when all men wear a white tie and a black tailcoat in the evening, the individual character of each man is made more important, not less; and a curious effect then occurs in mixed company. If each woman at the ball is carefully wearing something different, the different costumes are what you see first across the room, making a variable scene; but consequently the faces might as well be all the same, just as if the same doll were dressed in many different ways. When two women wear the same dress, however, the first thing you see is how different the actual women really look.

The Romantic movement was in fact already generating the notion of Woman as a creature who may appear in many guises but who always has the same nature. "Woman" became a sort of single primitive force, encountered by individual men in the form of dramatically varied samples which were nonetheless believed to be only superficially different, sisters under the differently colored skin. This notion was partly responsible for the marked division, in clothes of the later Romantic period, between masculine solidarity about uniform style and dim color, and a feminine diversity largely based on vigorous polychromy. Mid-nineteenth-century paintings by Frith and indeed by Monet and Manet show groups of multicolored ladies blooming like varieties of flowering shrubbery among sturdy, dun-colored, tree-trunk-like gentlemen with distinctive faces.

At the very beginning of the intense Neo-classic period, however, women followed the antique rule for color, and appeared for a time in Classical white, modified by a few natural hues for draped shawls and turbans, or for hats, shoes, gloves and parasols. The effect of all this artistically created natural simplicity was not just to show devotion to antique purity of form but obviously to intensify the erotic streak already evident in the Neo-classic art and taste that made so much of the completely described forms of the nude. Manners had abruptly changed along with the political situation, and crude behavior and sexual license became more publicly noticeable on both sides of the Channel. In high and low art, erotic intensity was well conveyed in a linear style with very little color, as the works of Flaxman, Blake, Gillray, Rowlandson, Fuseli, and indeed Goya demonstrate. Lush color makes nudes in art more beautiful and more realistic—but absence of color can certainly make them more *graphic*.

In France, a specifically erotic colorlessness had its own vogue, perhaps in imitation of English art. The fashionable artist Boilly made various semi-pornographic drawings in *grisaille*, showing the new revealing modes in action among the gallants and loose ladies of Paris, whose thin draperies were always more extreme than anything attempted in England. It is easy to see why the French found the new English tailored male figure compelling. In men's clothes no less than in women's thin muslin, it was not just antiquity but sexual attractiveness that the new tailoring conveyed. Its trace of country flavor also went well with the rude, free airs of lower-class grooms and coachmen, which could be all the more seductively adopted by elegant gentlemen. As with the Greek hero, part of the tailored hero's personal excellence was his physical desirability, another purely individual trait, now insisted on by smooth pantaloons in pale clinging materials.

FRENCH AND ENGLISH Neo-classicism show how similar forms may be used to express different ideas. The way the same Neo-classic formal revisions in art quickly and simultaneously affected fashion in France and in England demonstrates that a quick rise of a certain form in fashion initially reflects the power of the form itself, not the political idea it comes to embody. We have suggested that a certain fashion may often precede a shift in politics and cultural attitude, to show an esthetic, almost physical desire for basic change rather than to reflect new ideas after they arise. The new form is adopted first out of a desire to change an extant style in a way that satisfies the psyche first, by satisfying the eye without taking on the burden of rational excuses and political adhesions. A social and political meaning necessarily gets attached to the fashion afterwards, to rationalize the unconscious need; and later the meaning can seem to have been what forced the change.

But if the formal simplicities of antiquity looked wonderful to both the French and the English at the same time, at a period in history when they were so widely different in cultural situation and social aim, the need to adopt antique forms must have arisen out of neither the one nor the other set of current social ideals. It must have come from an esthetic longing common to both, without reference to any immediate political applications, a need to change the look of things into something radically old and new at once. Unmodified antique looks must have had a satisfying emotional meaning that was deeper than any society's current social references. The thrilling union of well-thumbed Classical form with a new raw sexuality, a new creative originality and a new brute truthfulness would certainly satisfy; and it would be easy to ally it later with any current potency, whether of finance, commerce, war or politics.

The erotic character of the new masculine mode in the first decade of the nineteenth century was intensified by its demanding qualities. The more simply fitted clothes of Baroque times had been easier to wear for everybody. Perfectly fitting clothes and neckwear now required elegant posture and movement, which had to look effortless since they were invoking and allegedly imitating nature. In the days of stiff doublets and ruffs, prescribed deportment was itself stiff, and nobody wearing them pretended to behave naturally, that is, slackly and undesignedly. But in the Neo-classic climate, the wearer showed his potency by the ease with which he seemed unaware of the difficulty of his clothes and exhibited a transcendent nonchalance.

As always, the tension created by such a fusion of opposites—the effortless effort—had a strong erotic charge in itself. It was another example of the kind of sexual heroism evident in the graceful female management of trains, hoopskirts, corsets and extreme high heels, as it once had been in the tight, trussed-up, padded and very short male doublets of the early Renaissance. In fact the appeal of the modern suit in our period is still its combined look of comfort and crispness, with its neat collar and tie that perpetually defy the forces of hot weather, hard work and high anxiety, its unruffled tailored envelope suggesting an invincible physical aplomb, including sexual. No sweat-suits, cycling gear, or wrinkled khakis can hope to convey such a superior level of ease.

IN ITS ORIGINAL Neo-classic or Dandy form, however, the modern masculine costume proved too extreme to do all its classicizing work at once, and to evoke the innate heroism of every man. Not only the corpulent but the seriously busy could not hold the perfectly natural Classical pose for very long. The fashion had begun among the seriously idle, some of whom had the leisure to align their physical behavior with the high artistic standard of the tailoring. Very soon it became obvious that modifications in the tailoring were necessary, to preserve the same high standard while demanding less contribution from the man himself. Idle or not, he should not be required to muster all the original creative zeal of the Brummellian pioneers. By 1815, trousers had largely replaced the sleek, demanding pantaloons, and men's arms and legs became similarly clad in smooth cylinders of yielding fabric. The modern "suit" was now in existence, meaning the unified abstraction of shape that is its defining characteristic; but it still did not have to be made of the same fabric for trousers and coat, except in evening dress. Waistcoats could also still be separate.

TROUSERS HAD BEEN another informal fashion that looked rather bunchy and sloppy the way the "frock" had done, until tailors refined and formalized them to match the smooth new abstraction made out of the country coat. The new, elegant trousers were often strapped under the instep for a more perfect vertical fit. By 1830, the "frock coat," an elegant version of the old modest country frock, had become correct for daytime wear in cities. Its full skirt and closed front concealed the crotch and created a clothed shape for business and professional men that was soberer than the original nude mode, with its explicit genital focus. Daytime coats thereafter all veiled the crotch; formal morning dress and evening wear kept to the older and nuder idea, until the tuxedo was invented to keep even the nocturnal male in harmony with his business self.

To compensate for the concealing coat, the cravat became more brilliant and more suggestive, gradually allowing itself both bright color and greater stiffness, and even later an exciting vertical thrust. The whole costume remained thoroughly erotic, but it became more abstract still. The foundation remained the Classical body and the relaxed but authoritative *contrapposto* of the Classical pose, with weight on one foot and an easily turning head. Hair might grow fairly long, but never so as to drag against the shoulders when the head turned. Knees and elbows pushed casually through the cloth, creating a few spare folds that echoed, with an austere and flattering rhythm, the easy dignity of the wearer's natural demeanor.

There is a more general esthetic background to the rise of the classic modern suit, a background created by the superior talent of all English decorative designers during the late eighteenth century and the early nineteenth—superior, that is, at producing the most enduringly desirable results. Among others, Robert Adam set a standard of design for furniture, interiors and houses that has perhaps been matched but never surpassed in its restrained use of past styles to form something both fresh and lasting. Georgian houses and household articles are still visually pleasing without apology or ideology.

The English practical designers of the period did not want to congeal the antique in perfect copies, like the French Empire replicas of Imperial Roman *sediae*. They insisted rather on an underlying esthetic virtue in Classical design that could be reconstituted in the form of useful modern tables and chairs showing the beauty of the natural wood, or staircases and sitting-rooms of spacious simplicity. English architects were in any case continuing to use a Palladian style untrammeled by Continental Rococo fancy; and practical domestic design showed a similar unpretentious clarity when Neo-classic ideals overtook it.

The tailors of England essentially attempted the same sort of remodelling during the same period; and they, too, had an English tradition of simplicity behind them, in contrast to the busier modes of France and Italy, and in keeping with other Nordic styles apparent in Holland, Russia, Germany and Scandinavia. Their Neo-classic version of the suit was a triumph for modernity much as the late Georgian house also was, something of which the grace and utility are fused and simultaneously evident. Like the houses and furniture, the new male costume was founded on both modern craft principles and antique ideals. Men's fashion made such flexible use of the old forms of dress that they were released instead of fixed in time, and given the freedom to survive and satisfy far into the unimagined future. English Neo-classic designers of both clothes and furniture thus followed the old sense of the word "original," meaning a creative new use of old sources.

For Georgian silver and furniture, which are detached from the body, no later modifications were necessary, and the actual antique objects are still used and prized even more than new versions, while closely imitated reproductions also serve very well. But clothes are fundamentally different; and no one now wears actually surviving Regency coats. Since fashionable clothes are not themselves impersonal Mirrors of Society but inseparable from the living organisms they cover, they have a relation to the mortal rhythm of actual lives and to personal fantasy that chairs can't share.

The clothes of long-dead generations are truly dead, except as curiosities; their only true later life is in the vigorous progeny they beget. People are now celebrating the vitality of the Regency suit by continuing to wear its direct descendant in the modern suit, still finding it to be an appropriate extension of their modern selves, still using it to create a bodily picture that satisfies the modern soul. The influence of Neo-classicism thus modernized men's clothes; but it was to take a century for women to catch up. It's therefore clear that the greatest Neo-classic contribution to costume history was not the celebrated draped white dress with the high waistline, made immortal in David's portraits, but the English tailored male, whose immortality is manifest in the continuing life of tailored suits among both men and women in the modern world.

READY-MADE MEN

IN ORDER TO KEEP pace with modern life, suits continued their stylistic modifications; but the most important later change in the new male costume was invisible. A revolution occurred in the way most suits were made, but in such a manner that their looks were essentially preserved. What became a different sort of object was nevertheless maintained as the same sort of costume, in which the noticeable changes kept their evolutionary rhythm. It was a mark of the essential modernity of

Caspar David Friedrich, *The Traveller Above the Sea of Fog,* German, 1818.

LEFT: Eugène Delacroix, *Baron Schwiter,* French, 1826–28. BELOW: John Everett Millais, *Portrait of John Ruskin,* English, 1854.

Romantic suited man, in a suitable setting. Opposite, the German hero faces the mists of the unknown, his suit both arming and denuding him properly to meet fate; the young French baron's suit (left) forms a sequence of dark mobile curves which flatter and strengthen his beauty, and thus put him in harmony with the elegant garden around him. The English sage (below) climbs among the wild rocks and torrents, his suit forming an intelligent visual abstraction of the chaotic forms in nature, out of which he makes order as he walks. All three salute the sky bareheaded, lending their free hair to the breeze and spray.

the look that this was possible. Ready-to-wear, mass-produced suits for the general public were created with as high a standard of design and finish as that set for bespoke tailoring.

Part of the revival of interest in Classical artifacts was an interest in Classical proportion, and a new interest in proportion altogether as the basis of satisfactory practical design. Tailoring for men had never before made use of this principle, because all clothes had been made to personal measure. Tailors only needed to keep track of individual measurements, not to draw conclusions about general male proportions. For each client, tailors kept a single strip of tape with his name on it, marked with labelled notches indicating the length of his forearm, the distance around his neck, the width between his shoulders, or whatever was needed for the fit of his garment. The client's suit would be cut accordingly, altering a very general pattern to match the notches on his individual tape.

The tape-measure, marked out in impersonal and universal inches that might apply its measurements to all and then compare the results, was only invented in about 1820. It was used for the express purpose of making well-fitting suits for many unmeasured men at once, using a principle of common rules for masculine physical proportions. Many new measuring schemes were invented by skilled and experienced tailors for the creation of variable patterns that would make ready-to-wear suits desirably well-fitting. Since Classical bodily proportions were part of the fiction behind Neo-classic suits in the first place, the plan served both an imaginative ideal and a very practical commercial purpose. Neo-classic suits were originally designed to augment chests and shoulders just a little, to suggest natural heroism with very subtle artifice, and "perfect fit" was already a slightly fictional matter, even for bespoke examples. This fact helped make ready-made production easier to manage and gave it predictably excellent results.

It gradually became clear that a great many men with a particular chest measurement would be very likely to have a similar width of shoulder, a similar waist size, and a similar distance down the center of the back between neck and waist, and similar lengths of arm and leg. Ready-to-wear suit-coats and trousers on the new classic model could make use of these generalities; but they would be given the extremely apt help of Neo-classic generalities, created by the delicate selective shaping and padding that had been designed to improve anybody's figure. Thus you could buy yourself a ready-made Classical body that fit beautifully and suited you perfectly, and that could even seem to improve your individual face. Maybe the trouser-length could be adjusted just a little before delivery.

As may be surmised, excellent ready-made suits were originally an American phenomenon. They were already well on their way to phenomenal success in the 1820's, when English gentlemen would personally never consider wearing them. Observers in the New World, however, remarked that American gentlemen, who had always quickly adopted elegant English fashion, were already becoming very hard to distinguish from American farmers, shop-keepers and artisans who were appearing in the park or at church in well-cut, well-fitting ready-made town clothes.

These were the first ready-to-wear garments with a real similarity to those worn at the highest level of fashion. They were possible because the highest level of skill in fashionable tailoring had gone into their conception and design, a design that was originally meant for exactly such variation as ready-to-wear production required. Common clothes were for the first time truly raised to the level of elegance, not condemned to being debased versions of unattainably fine things, nor low-seeming things to begin with. For two centuries, ready-made male garments had been irredeemably humble objects, mostly unfitted pants, shirts and jackets for laborers and sailors; now they rivalled the festive wear of the upper classes. And this new situation, like earlier inspired sartorial moments, was a wholly masculine enterprise.

Ready-to-wear garments for women came into existence, but the elegant ones were all mantles, cloaks or capes that required no fitting at all, and hats and bonnets. Plain skirts were sold, too, but nothing ready-made could challenge the carefully trimmed and fitted made-to-measure dresses of nineteenth-century women. Well before 1820, the standards of craftsmanship for female dressmaking had steadily risen to keep pace with the increasing simplicity of all material taste and the new desire for formal clarity in all fashionable clothes. The superior cut and fit of dresses, not just the richness of their surface, had come to be what demonstrated their superior elegance; and dresses had to continue being individually cut, because they continued to be closely fitted over corsets that were made and laced to fit the individual figure. Only toward the end of the nineteenth century, when corsets were also ready-made, were ready-made dresses, suits and shirtwaists considered acceptable. Before that, dressmakers at all levels made women's clothes to order, or they were made at home. We read of Lucy Snowe, Charlotte Brontë's poor schoolteacher, having her dresses made; and we read of Jo March making the dresses for her whole family of sisters.

It must be added here that the cut, fit and general look of a man's ready-made, off-the-rack suit (then as now) might certainly be clumsy, unseemly, or ridiculous. That would in part depend on the technical skill and artisanal responsibility of the mass-producing tailor and his assistants, on the commercial responsibility of the furnisher and his salesmen, and thus on the price paid. But, then as now, it would also largely depend on the self-knowledgeable and discriminating eye of the purchaser himself. The custom tailor's client doesn't need any visual taste; the tailor will have it for him, and won't let the client leave the shop unless his suited looks are a credit to the firm. But the ready-to-wear customer's looks are his own responsibility. He must cultivate his own eye with care, for the sake of his visual credit in the eye of beholders. The American farmers who looked just like gentlemen in 1820 were obviously the ones who knew how.

During the course of the nineteenth century, the prestige of bespoke tailoring was maintained in England and France, and European ready-to-wear men's clothes were never as well-made as American ones. The highest note of elegance everywhere, however, was no longer being struck by the look of leisured refinement but by the look of seriousness, a flavor certainly not unsuitable for nobility and gentry but actually invented by serious merchant princes as far back as the Renaissance. Modern men did not invent the restrained look—it had been one feature of all Renaissance fashion—but its intense revival provided an excellent flavor for nineteenth-century masculine concerns, and went very well with the simplified forms of modern male fashion, and with the new possibilities of ready-to-wear elegance.

Severe probity once again became the sartorial message even of kings, and bespoke tailoring relied for its distinction on subtle cut and the fine texture of its dim fabrics even more than on fit, as the fashion in masculine bodily shape became less emphatic. Colors for men became more somber; but it was still the case until late in the century that formal

daytime wear for urban gentlemen, whether they were dukes or solici-
tors, businessmen or politicians, was usually made using different cloth
for the coat and pants. The requisite dark, smooth frock coat might have
lighter trousers, dark morning coats were worn with striped trousers,
and the waistcoat might be made of still another fabric. A certain infor-
mality might also inhere in the use of bright checks for trousers and
waistcoat only, while the coat remained sober, just the way casual pants
may nowadays be worn with an elegant jacket to indicate leisure, not
duty.

What we now call suits existed, but they were emphatically informal, or else noticeably lower-class. The gentleman's "lounge-suit," all
parts made of a single fabric, had originally been intended for leisured
country life and very private city use, to be worn only at home and
among intimates. It was made of a soft, tweedy or checked material with
a rather short and easy coat, and waistcoat to match. Its slightly rough
surface, comparatively light color, and especially its one-fabric form suggested a sort of tame-animal costume, a cosy set of garments meant to
have a relaxing effect on the wearer, to relieve him of his frock-coated
public dignity and make him accessible. A gentleman might travel in his
comfortable lounge-suit; but it was certainly not acceptable at the bank
or the firm, nor at church, nor at highly formal social events in the daytime, nor for anything at all in the evening.

During the same period, however, the farmers and laborers of the
later nineteenth century were all wearing ready-to-wear versions of just
such suits for all dressed-up occasions, and so were shop-assistants and
other city workers of all kinds, often in strong serviceable fabric and
dark colors. Well below the high levels of fashion where daytime cut-
aways and full evening dress were commonly worn, ordinary three-piece
suits were universal formal wear for every sort of very Common Man.
Plenty of photographs show villagers and factory-hands in their tailored
festive best.

In big cities, severe frock coats and morning coats with striped
pants—both costumes demanding rigid headgear, stiff neckwear, and
gloves—were gradually abandoned between the two World Wars, although formal morning dress was preserved in the City of London and
elsewhere for ceremonial daytime moments. We still see the cutaway and
striped pants at private weddings, and among diplomats and statesmen.

The lowly lounge-suit meanwhile became the all-purpose formal costume for men of this century, whatever their class or occupation. After the Second World War, the expensive made-to-measure version was refined, dimmed and smoothed out, and generally enhanced in the public mind as the new standard image of the elegant male.

Ordinary male citizens naturally continued to wear mass-produced versions in all price brackets. It was during this period, when similar suits began to suit everybody, that ferocious sneering about ready-made suits began to seep into snobbish rhetoric. In life as well as literature, "ill-fitting" and similar terms would describe the modest suits of persons with the wrong moral qualities, to signal their emotional maladroitness and instability, even their unscrupulousness, and automatically consign them to lower levels of being. "Off-the-rack" itself became a term of deep opprobrium. As we know, ready-to-wear suits can fit perfectly and be made of beautiful stuff; but the rhetoric persists, even now.

The lounge-suit's rise into urban elegance offers a fine example of fashion at work in familiar ways. We saw how country clothes were made into formal city wear in the years following 1800. In the early twentieth century, a similar modish urban desire to combine a startling air of nonchalance with a reference to plebeian practice promoted lounge-suit-wearing as the new chic and daring thing for fashionable men about town. Three-piece one-fabric suits were then almost the equivalent of modern jeans—something not only officially informal but notably vulgar, quite out of place at the office or at lunch with senior associates, and nevertheless increasingly worn in a rebellious spirit by confident and privileged young men. It certainly caught on, just like the earlier mode, and the later one.

The black dinner-jacket, or tuxedo, was also first invented a hundred years ago in easygoing America as an informal coat to go with black evening trousers, something cosy for family and close friends. Now it has become publicly formal evening dress, somewhat austere and ceremonial. The black tailcoat worn with white tie, white waistcoat, stiff shirt and silk hat, once prescribed for all gentlemen in the evening in all private or public places, including theaters and restaurants, is still worn on certain formal festive occasions; but it is now mostly seen on performers, many of them female.

White tie and tails has become a purely traditional costume, no longer a necessary part of every well-off male city-dweller's wardrobe. If conventional men's suits eventually follow the same path, we may finally see them only at weddings, or on men in highly specialized occupations, or only on female cabaret performers. We may notice that in the middle of the nineteenth century, when gentlemen all went to the ball in white tie and tails, the footmen all wore brocade coats, breeches, and powdered wigs—gentleman's gear of a century before. At a modern restaurant, you may already see the headwaiter in black tie and dinner-jacket, and the patron in denims, sweatshirt and running shoes.

THE ONCE AND FUTURE SUIT

MALE COSTUME since the Neo-classic revolution thus shows how the subversive principle operates. At first, the revolutionary new male tailoring proliferated in a thousand ways, both vertically and laterally. Victorian gentlemen became just as good at elaborate clothing as their wives and daughters, owning many different custom-made tailored garments with many accessories for many sorts of social and professional occasion, many of them uncomfortable and demanding, some of them sporting and easier to wear, but all of them equally complicated. Simple lounge-suits for the population in the meantime also proliferated in many styles, colors and textures, and naturally in many degrees of quality.

Besides suits for plebeian weddings and Sunday, however, workclothes were made in the new form. In Realist French and English paintings and illustrations of the nineteenth century, you can see fieldlaborers in trousers of rough wool or corduroy worn with tailored jackets or waistcoats over colored or striped shirts, where breeches and smocks would have appeared two generations before. In the United States, jeans and overalls joined the group.

When every man was in a version of tailored clothes—at the ball, in the office, on the prairie, or down the mineshaft—the system clearly needed an emotional and visual shaking up, especially if the formal principles were to be retained. And so it has gone, with sporting gear, laboring gear, and of course military and criminal gear arriving in the drawing-room or at the opera or the restaurant to startle the eye and unsettle the feelings. With the advent of cinema and television, all sorts of outdated, historical, theatrical and foreign motifs have entered the masculine picture, and the whole society has liberated its male sartorial possibilities so they may often coexist and interpenetrate. A white tuxedo and a purple sweat-suit might now be seen at the same occasion without seeming remarkable, just the way truly disparate modes may be seen on women in the same room.

There has nevertheless been a single limiting male principle in all this, the same one women have persistently copied since the beginning. You can see it by noticing what men don't wear, with all their recent variety. First of all they tend not to combine different programs, as women often do; that is, he won't wear the sweatpants *with* the white tuxedo jacket, as women's fashion indicates she might—unless he's in a very self-conscious thrift-shop mode. Most men's dress continues to express a greater sense of visual boundaries than women's, perhaps of esthetic propriety, I would say even a keener sense of modern design, based on the notion that a single costume fulfills a single esthetic purpose, and requires a single idea to unify its visibly separate parts.

Notably, Western men still don't want to wear drapery, gowns and robes or shawls and veils. The body itself must remain articulated, never swathed, and be unified only by the idea, not by loose fabric. Men don't wear skirts either, partly for the same reason—pants may be very baggy, but they are emphatically still trousers. If skirts ever come to be commonly worn by Western men, they might have the character of the kilt or the ancient Roman military skirt, later copied in the Renaissance— something quite short and heavily swinging, to show the legs and allow them full action, and also to carry the right robust Western flavors. The long wrapped sarongs now visible on television as normal male gear in Africa might catch on temporarily, but I believe not generally— old habits, as I have repeatedly said, die very hard. In the West since the Middle Ages, draped and enveloping clothing is emphatically non-masculine, except for priests or monks whose dress carefully plays down the corporeal.

I would claim that the naked male body, coherent and articulated, must still be the ghostly visual image and the underlying formal suggestion made by any ordinary male Western costume, however closely the surface is covered, just as it was made by the suit of plate armor or the first Neo-classic suit. The modern suit survives partly because among all the more showily revealing varieties of current male dress, it has kept its ability to make that nude suggestion.

THE CLASSIC MAN'S SUIT continues to evolve without permitting any extreme violations, it keeps its traditional sober beauty and subtle surfaces, and women still normally do not wear it. They have, of course, several times shown that they can; but they usually don't. They wear many approximations and creative versions; but the complete classical suit with shirt and tie is still mostly men's property. And it is partly because of this that some men have begun to feel a bit stuck with it, in the sexually fluid atmosphere that fashion now reflects. The suit remains the uniform of official power, not manifest force or physical labor—it suggests diplomacy, compromise, civility, and physical self-control, none of which are presently in the fashionable ascendant. The Secretary of State ought to wear it, certainly; but nowadays it is obvious that not everyone wants to sport the look of avoiding emotional explosions or open conflict at all costs.

The suit does not itself constrict the body the way armor or Renaissance doublets did; it is an easy-fitting sheath. But it hides the body's whole surface quite thoroughly, and it usually offers its ensemble of lines, colors and shapes with discretion. Consequently the suit now has the reputation of being inexpressive, in an era of trained muscles and near nudity, to say nothing of political protest, sexual revolution and ethnic assertion, besides all the resources of theatrical and cinematic glamor everyone now may draw on.

Suits are obviously not really inexpressive; they express classical *modernity*, in material design, in politics, and in sexuality. In their pure form, they express a confident adult masculinity, unflavored with either violence or passivity. The suit reflects purposeful development, not quixotic inspiration; it has the modern look of carefully simplified dynamic abstraction that has its own strong sexual appeal. In society it began as an apt visual foil for the vivid and variable fanciful inventions worn by women, and it still does—but only if the women's garments match the men's with respect to careful conception, fit and construction. Today, a modest gathering at which men really obey the "black tie" rule, for example, will often have an embarrassingly unequal look: the women will look dowdy in tired or out-of-date evening dresses, or else insufficiently festive in nice daytime wear, whereas the men will all look marvelous in their dinner-jackets, however old their fashion is and whatever their degree of shabbiness.

In the daytime, classic male suits can look less well when juxtaposed to much post-modern feminine clothing, with its throwaway, thrown-together, fragmented character and its deliberately careless, ephemeral look, often unconstructed, unfitted and essentially unconceived. When juxtaposed to those effects, a man's suit can start to seem stuffy; but it can also, of course, make post-modern women seem sloppy and anarchic and lacking in discrimination, depending on the occasion and the point of view. Suits do have, as I said at the beginning, a way of looking superior.

A man's suit naturally makes a good foil for classic female suits, since those were invented to harmonize with the male version, and for other classic forms of modern female ensemble—dresses in one or two pieces, skirt-and-jacket combinations of all sorts. Such suit-supplementing garments, not all of them suits, are worn by female professionals of all kinds, politicians and television announcers, by women in boardrooms, courtrooms, and in countless offices; and they are lately getting some of the same disparaging rhetorical treatment as male suits, even while they continue as fundamental staples of modern female wardrobes.

Since this mainstream feminine mode is the adult female version of the male suit, its brand of sexuality is similarly adult and essentially self-respecting, rather than exuberant, boastful, infantine or perverse. Its eroticism is unfailingly discreet, and it is therefore inescapably respectable. Consequently this mainstream modern mode for women has lost a certain public éclat, especially in the fashion press, which must uphold the subversive element in fashion, and seek to praise the forms of novelty that seem reliably disruptive and playful. Modern classic simplicity can appear to betray the present spirit of extreme free expression for all, in all contexts; but the tailored, discreet mode for both sexes is visibly holding its own without the need of fanfare. In the Haute Couture it remains a constant challenge for the best creative talent.

Plainly the male suit is no longer universal for men. It nevertheless retains its look of upholding standards, and therefore it retains its prestige, along with its special brand of confident male sexuality. Feminizing variations made upon its basic shapes and textures, invented chiefly for use by women during the last fifty years, along with the new elements brought to it by designers who have worked for both sexes, such as Bill Blass, Gianni Versace, Giorgio Armani and lately Donna Karan, have deeply affected male fashion by demonstrating the possible future development of the suit in a changed cultural climate. But all this invention has gone forward without ever actually killing or dislodging the classic male suit itself.

If suits should prove vulnerable to real corruption, so that pure examples could only eventually be acquired by determined cultists and rabid preservationists, for whom a small number would still be expensively made, then we might admit its day was really over. But so far, no such thing. Excellent ready-to-wear suits are being sold in great numbers in every major city, and exquisite bespoke tailoring is by no means dead. It is in fact still setting the standard for the ready-to-wear business, so that suit merchants will assure you that their product is indistinguishable from custom-made examples except on close inspection.

IV. MODERNITY

WORTH AND HIS EFFECTS

WE HAVE SEEN how distant the sartorial relations between men and women became during the course of the eighteenth century, and we can watch the distance increase during the first two-thirds of the nineteenth. The worlds of masculine tailoring and feminine dressmaking were quite divided, and men and women were separate sorts of visual being. With the advent of Charles Frederick Worth on the Parisian scene, a dramatic new element was entering these relations: clothes could increasingly suggest that women were not only creatures quite different from men, but essentially the creations of men. Worth was not responsible for this perception, but his masculine presence and influence in the realm of appearances helped to crystallize it.

Worth first established himself in the dry-goods business in Paris, and he gradually set up a dress-design department as a sideline of that before inventing his couture business in 1858, which combined both. He became the first "man-milliner," boldly invading the domain that guarded the mysteries of the boudoir, concerning himself with the actual details of feminine dress in a world that had been wholly feminine for a century and a half. His advent in that sphere produced considerable shock, ridicule and disapproval, since before him, dresses were commonly designed, made and embellished by female dressmakers in ateliers staffed by female workers, and small repairs or changes were made at home by the lady herself or her maid.

Materials and trimmings were sold separately in dry-goods shops often owned and staffed by men, but male influence was still discreetly remote from the actual creative process, certainly from its manual aspects. The creation of a dress was moreover a joint feminine enterprise in which the client herself could have a large part, coordinating the separate offerings of the fabric store with the suggestions and capacities of the dressmaker, and following her own taste and personal ideas at each stage. Just as in past centuries, the whole matter was private if not secret, and the public, especially the masculine public, was not supposed to be aware of the actual methods for achieving the final effect, nor to know the names of the dressmaker and suppliers.

It must always be borne in mind that until the last third of the nineteenth century, which also included the establishment of creative male couturiers, there was virtually no ready-to-wear fashion for women, only outer garments and headwear. What was not custom-made was home-made or second-hand. In fact most women, rich or poor, knew how to sew or understood sewing—huge numbers made their living by it—and this meant that personal technical adjustments to all details and levels of modishness were a matter of course. For women themselves, if not for the men who gazed on them, their clothes were no mystery, created in unknown places by unfamiliar processes. Clothes and their construction were an intimate domestic matter for most women, who might not be gifted in cutting and fitting but who would nevertheless know exactly how their own dresses were put together. They might themselves sew interminably for the household, hemming sheets and towels and making undergarments along with doing all the mending. Embroidery was done in front of company; all the rest of it was standard woman's work.

Tailoring for men, on the other hand, was indeed a mystery to the customer (unless he was himself a tailor), with the whole technical operation undertaken by superior craftsmen entirely out of the client's sight and knowledge, once he indicated what sort of thing he wanted and was measured for it. Worth when he appeared, and his male colleagues thereafter, seemed to be wrenching dressmaking out of the ordinary knowledgeable female hands that had properly dealt with its intimate aspects, and shifting it into the lofty realm of male vision and expertise, where master-tailors reigned. Male artistic privileges would now seem, shockingly, to permit a man to mold and drape a costume directly onto a female client's submissive body, to exercise his creative talent on her physical being.

Tailoring establishments for men provided all the materials along with the finished product, the two having long seemed obviously inextricable. Men didn't brood at home over fashion plates, and then go to several different fabric stores and study many varieties of texture and fiber, and shop around for different colors for facings, and compare the thicknesses of ornamental braid or the sizes of buttons, all in connection with going separately to the tailor's shop and ordering a suit. The design of a suit would moreover be a matter of variation on an established form, the variant often consisting only of a new fabric or trim suggested and provided by the tailor himself. His shop would then see to all the results from beginning to end.

Worth, an Englishman with the tradition of English tailoring behind him, got from it the simple idea of inventing a line of possible garments for possible clients in connection with the fabrics and trimmings available in his shop. And in this way he became the first real "designer," who makes up a group of finished compositions entirely out of his own imagination, which encompasses every aspect of how they look, just like that of an artist. The client only needs to choose which of his visions she wishes to become.

The male designer of clothes has ever since been a figure of enormous prestige among women, a prestige based on the achievements of those who have primarily enhanced female attractions, both in men's eyes and in their own, rather than concentrating on their own inventiveness—the ones who have seemed to design the woman herself, to remold her nearer to the heart's desire. The most admired are now those who can do it for many women at once, creating ready-to-wear modes that appear to bring out the unique charms of each purchaser.

It was obvious that when women were creating all their own effects with the assistance of dressmakers, no couturière had anywhere near the prestige of a male artist. Gross failures of visual taste, the result of inept collaborations between a willful female client and an obedient or untalented female artisan, could sometimes lead to awkward and disharmonious effects not possible to men with good tailors. Fashionable women might look ridiculous; fashionable men never did. Vast freedom of visual choice is always difficult to manage without a strong and sure eye to give guidance, internal or external. Women's expanded range of options could sometimes confound them, then as now.

But if a strong-minded male designer with an artist's eye and the hand of a good tailor could be in charge of feminine taste in clothes, the women who chose to be dressed by him would be prevented from letting their vulgarity or vanity or obsessiveness or perhaps their timidity and dimness of view get the better of them. They could rely on his superior male understanding of their visual possibilities, naturally sparked by underlying male desire. Worth's original success was consequently phenomenal, and not surprising. He used his own pretty wife as a mannequin, taking her out in public in his dresses to convey the quality of his imagination about women and clothes. His actual designs do show much more imaginative verve than the offerings of feminine dressmakers from his date and just before. They look as if he were indeed a dedicated male fantasist inventing female creatures in exquisite detail.

The sartorial situation thus created in mid-nineteenth-century Paris by Worth's success, and carried on for a century after him, did have strong parallels in the artistic world of the moment. There, other imaginative men were creating unforgettable women out of their heads, women who seemed more real and more attractive, more fierce and compelling than real ones—Anna K. and Emma B., Carmen and Nana, Daisy and Isabel and Olive, Tess Durbeyfield and Lizzie Hexam, all fleshed out with distinctive physical selves. Painters had of course always been engaged in the same enterprise, from Botticelli and Rubens on to Ingres and Courbet, for each of whom the live model simply provided the chance to expand and expound the perfect texture of the painter's fantasy.

Worth only confirmed the idea that the most interesting women are formed out of the precise imaginative longings of men. This idea is certainly not wholly unwelcome to women themselves, laden as it has been with all its ancient eroticism ever since Ovid wrote the story of Pygmalion, or since the original violent myth of Athena's birth. Male artists' female creations are not always erotic creatures; but the whole process is itself erotic, and actual women have repeatedly responded to that. To be a man's creation is to participate intimately in his sexuality, whatever kind of creature you turn out to be; it's a thrilling and dangerous prospect. And so it seemed to Worth's clients, as it still does to those of Christian Lacroix. Fashion, as we have established, is founded on risk.

There was nothing modern about the idea of men making women's clothes—we saw them doing it for centuries in the past. In the old days, however, the client was always primary and her tailor an obscure artisan, perhaps talented but perhaps not. She had her own ideas like any patron, there were no fashion plates, and the tailor was simply at her service, perhaps with helpful suggestions about what others were wearing. Beginning in the late nineteenth century, with the hugely successful rise of the artistic male couturier, it was the designer who became pre-eminent, and the client elevated by his inspired attention. In a climate of admiration for male artists and their female creations, the dress-designer first flourished as the same sort of creator. Instead of the old rule that dressmaking is a craft, a modern connection between dress-design and art was invented that had not been there before. This notion was reinforced by Worth, who seems to have thought of himself that way and behaved with theatrical artistic arrogance, and later by Jacques Doucet in a very different vein.

Doucet was a cultivated connoisseur of art and a friend of many painters—he was the first owner of Picasso's *Les Demoiselles d'Avignon* —and his suave, refined dresses suggested the elegance of eighteenth-century salons. They radiated not just the heavy power of money but the volatile power of rare intelligence and taste. Women dressed by him could feel wittier and more intrinsically charming; Worth's clients felt adorned and fortunate, like princesses. All of this contributed to the new idea that a dress-designer *ought* to be a man, someone like Tolstoy or Flaubert, with a great talent for inventing women who would captivate the male imagination. An important element in all this has continued to be the fact that clothing is always fused with the wearer in the eye of the observer, as we have suggested. Women whose most dazzling effects are created by designers can count on getting the immediate credit and all the deep responses for themselves. The women created by authors and painters get them, too; the best fantasies breathe with their own life.

But by mid-century, the Romantic separation of the sexes had also intensified the pernicious feeling, strengthened by great art and literature but promulgated by popular myths, that women aren't ordinary persons, each naturally a human mixture. Females routinely acquired the quality of fitting into certain neat projections of male belief, each woman subject to instant generalization about all women, or all women of a certain sort. Women became separately catalogued as saints, victims or harlots, angels, demons or soulless sprites, personifications of nature's ferocious power or of divine love, of perversity or wisdom, of comfort or infernal vengeance—all without any natural psychological shading or complex moral texture. As physical presences in Romantic times, women consequently were expected to look like detailed concrete visions, in one style or another, of men's abstract and well-categorized fears and dreams about the female sex.

The newly arrived male couturiers could fit right into the scheme, as the appropriate costume designers for those women who felt themselves, consciously or not, to be living on a stage or inside a frame as players, working hard to fulfill masculine expectations to their own advantage. The period was also known for producing the *grandes horizontales,* the famous courtesans, living fantasies whose greatest renown derived from how much they cost to maintain, of which a good deal always went to the dressmaker. The male couturier's work could make any client into just such an unaccountable being, conjured out of drifting and iridescent silk gauze or carved out of seductively glittering jet and black velvet, with all the surface magic implying hidden pleasures and dangers that were clearly worth the visible costs. Just as in the theater, magnificent apparitions would be invisibly sustained by hidden yards of stiffened buckram and horsehair, and ultimately held in place by a substructure of steel, canvas and whalebone. Knowledge of these unseen devices only spiced the contemplation of the vision.

It should be noted that adept female dressmakers certainly continued in the profession after the arrival of Worth in 1858; but he raised the stakes and set the standard higher than it had ever been, an advanced standard both for imaginative cut and for dramatic forms of display, some of them relying on a daring new simplicity—a male standard, obscurely supported by the tailoring tradition, which is committed to formal integrity and purity of effect. Translated into a woman's dress in the Romantic mode, such a purity only underlined male ideas that a woman must be all damnation or all redemption, either a siren or a virgin: a white muslin dress might have one artless cascade of white roses and no other ornament, a fiery red brocade might have a sinuous applied pattern suggesting snakes.

Despite their delighted submission to the masculine creative process, after having laboriously arranged things for themselves for two centuries, some women began to feel altogether too invented, and many began to hate it bitterly. The middle of the nineteenth century had already seen the first wave of practical modern feminism, which arose partly and pointedly in connection with the abolition-of-slavery movement in the United States. Dress reform was a natural concomitant to this, although it had its own trajectory. The fanciful details of "Fashion" itself were never originally attributed to male tyranny, even by women, but to female idiocy, as they consistently had been ever since women began to dress women.

During all that time, between 1700 and 1860, women despised for dressing fashionably could not be seen as unwilling or unconscious slaves to a huge industrialized fashion business, nor to the spite of male couturiers, as they came to be in this century. Outcry instead often arose against the exploitation of the thousands of female needleworkers employed by elegant made-to-order businesses, the poor girls who struggled for low pay in bad conditions to finish all the complex creations on time. Women who made themselves look ridiculous in fashion's name, or who spent excessive amounts of thought, time and money on it, and who ordered many things on very short notice without ever considering the poor workwomen, were thought to be the victims of limited education and stunted morals, not of men's wishes, nor even of fashion itself.

Understanding of unconscious motivation was lacking, and female dress reformers at mid-century despised the extreme vagaries of fashion

for being stupid, primitive, even barbaric, and having the effect of lending women those qualities, or else of making them seem like willful
children or venal mountebanks. The delicate, hard-to-manage and wonderfully useless details of feminine fashion could seem to confirm the
already compromised position of adult female intelligence. Some
reform-minded women—then as now—felt that its creative pleasures had
to be altogether sacrificed.

The problem was the strongly ambiguous and ambivalent nature of
feminine dress. Many right-thinking men were very vocal, and had been
for centuries, about the horridly unnatural folly of cosmetics, constriction, and all sorts of extra furbelows; but most men still responded to
them with ready sexual feeling and emotional excitement. Many
women had the same responses, even to the whalebone. Nobody forth-
rightly defended the erotic and imaginative virtues of fashion itself except for male authors in France—Balzac, a great creator of women in
the first half of the century, was particularly eloquent about the poetic
force of feminine finery; and indeed no less so about masculine elegance. So were Stendhal and Baudelaire.

But early feminist objections in England and America were never
made to fashion as a male conspiracy, only to the male restriction of female minds that confined women to such allegedly unwholesome preoccupations. Among reformers, feminine fashion itself was rather seen as
feminine folly in material form, female weakness made manifest.
Women, after all, were making the hats and dresses as well as wearing
them. Male tailoring, even with all its mad impeccabilities and formalities, was never seen as weak. It was clear that men possessed the secret
of dressing in a way that made them look both serious and sexually
attractive.

But women who adopted male clothes or heavily masculinized
clothes could not strike the right note that way: they might look serious,
but they couldn't be taken seriously if they also looked somehow falsi-
fied or too willfully unappetizing. Perversely negative effects may startle,
but they always fail to persuade. The grim costumes worn by some
"Platform Women" were hopelessly ineffective as serious female clothes;
they added no force to the reformers' message because they looked as
if they were awkwardly suppressing truths, not demonstrating them.
Amelia Bloomer's celebrated costume, invented in 1851, had bypassed

male details in favor of slightly Oriental ones, to keep feminine flavor intact; but it lacked harmony, tacking a convenient but bizarre bottom onto a conventional top, and it couldn't revolutionize the feminine scheme honestly enough to make it manifestly serious either.

In the imitation-male style, eroticism and frivolity were only intensified by the look of severely tailored jackets artfully molded to feminine torsos, and female riding habits continued to be notoriously sexy in their mimicry of men—no new sort of general female reality was to be found in upper-class sports clothes. But the modern impulse in women's fashion to look toward male costume for its esthetically superior and formally integrating qualities, not just for its possible feminine charms, had already begun by the 1850's. This eventually had to mean women not dressing as men, but finding a female way to wear clothes that look both sexually interesting and ordinarily serious—actual not fictional—at the same time, the way men did. It took several generations to achieve this.

After Worth's success in the 1860's and the later rise of French male fashion designers, fashion for women began to show its role in sexual politics, not just in the display of class distinction or in the revelation of female vanity. Women came gradually to believe that they had been helping to fictionalize themselves, not just innocently adorning their persons. In avidly pursuing such a questionable goal, cultivated and respectable women might moreover have to rub shoulders with unlettered and vulgar courtesans in the same male designer's establishment; a common desire to be expensively created by a master could produce humiliating confrontations.

France was everywhere known to be the home of eroticism. The French male sexual imagination, so well deployed in dramas and novels or in poems and pictures, could now be seen blatantly at work in the realm of feminine dress, making the same sexual fictions out of living women. With such perception came even stronger protests against fashionable dress itself, with the new hidden implication that it was a pernicious masculine invention, sinfully sexy and French, that somehow helped take honest reality away from women—although this was not part of the public rhetoric.

The protest was naturally not French, but arose in sober Protestant countries viewing the phenomenon from a cultural distance, even while

Worth's clientele was international. In France itself, an unbroken tradition going back to the fifteenth century protected male or female fashion from ever being counted as the enemy of adult reason and virtue. It was assumed that strong sexuality, intellect and moral force could be smoothly blended in complex expressions of sartorial self-respect. Success in this would moreover mark an increase and not a loss of honor for persons of either sex in any class. Elegance, meaning a manifest concern for successful esthetic and erotic effects, was considered a proper quality for anybody's clothes, for worker's dress or servant's dress.

But in England and America, as well as in Germany, groups with names like the Rational Dress Society were formed to inaugurate new kinds of clothes founded on an ideal of Good Sense and designed expressly for women. "Sensible" ways for women to dress were advocated in the stubborn belief that feminine fashion itself could be escaped altogether, and that true beauty in female clothing could and should be rationally established. If this were done, it would allow women to be beautifully dressed and manifestly intelligent at the same time—a condition that many thought was impossible, if the subversively erotic displays of women's fashion were allowed to flourish. What was entirely forgotten was that male dress was equally the product of fantasy, a deeply erotic fashionable expression just like the female version. But men's clothes had long been striking the eye in a different way, appearing somehow naturally sensible in themselves, just as they had been carefully designed to do.

The complicated abstract phenomena of male fashion were not subject to general reform; only females were seen as needing rescue. Male dress might be seen by an individual esthete such as Oscar Wilde to be too stark for real beauty—he advocated going back to the Cavalier days of lace, velvet and loose hair for men. On the other hand, George Bernard Shaw suggested replacing elegant tailoring with knitted woolen tunics and breeches for health and comfort, and giving up beauty altogether. But these were eccentric personal notions, not movements. The reality of men, sexual and otherwise, was obviously quite well expressed in the male tailoring that had been evolving since 1800.

Feminine trappings were now seen to *hinder* the action of female reason, health, morality and intellect, as they never had been seen to do in earlier centuries. Although "Fashion" had been just as extreme before

Worth, during the hundred and fifty years when women were in charge of it, using plenty of high heels, big skirts and stiff stays, the most energetic and effective objections to hoops and corsets and all the rest of it came *after* Worth's success, and the inauguration of the Haute Couture as another serious masculine institution. Health, good esthetic principles, common sense and other vigorously reasonable notions were then brought resoundingly to bear by reformers, clearly to combat the powerful and pernicious force of male sexual fantasy. This was felt to be really threatening, in a way no simple feminine fripperies could possibly seem. Nobody was actively considering the linked role of female sexual fantasy at all, nor as yet the creative and positive power of sexual fantasy itself, felt but so far not acknowledged except in literature and art.

REFORMING WOMEN

REFORM ON THE BASIS of good sense was, of course, an ill-conceived and losing battle. Real change in what women wore could only occur when all unconscious fantasy changed its theme, and specifically female aspects of it were given fuller play in the fashion recipe; and that indeed eventually began to occur. Good sense in the form of more courageous esthetic decisions did come to affect women's clothes, originally under Worth's influence. More interesting female fantasy entered the world of fashion design around the end of the century, after Worth's death; and a great deal of the effect turned on new uses of male methods of dress that worked without sacrificing feminine custom. A positive re-modelling of form had to enhance the basic shape of the body, just as in the male dress of 1800. It wouldn't work simply to inhibit the old feminine details.

The idea of making women seem as real as men had to include visibly preserving and encouraging their own sense of femaleness, and keeping them attractive to themselves, self-aware and self-possessed.

Even before the turn of the century, under new pressure to project female reality rather than male fantasy, male designers and tailors for women had already begun to use feminine tailored clothes in variable ways, adapting the themes of riding dress to urban walking and travelling in trains and buses, but without invoking the look of a provocatively false man. At the same time, female designers entered the profession, with new ideas quite different from those expressed in the confections of Romantic dressmakers.

Between 1900 and 1912, women's clothes, which had been taking up more room than men's ever since the 1700's, were gradually reduced in scale so that the dressed bodies of men and women appeared equal in physical scope. Women's clothes also began to aim at creating a visual unity of bodily form, and the disappearance of emphatic breasts and hips was part of the trend. Corsetry was not abandoned, but it gradually changed its character. The new corsetting first concentrated mainly on suppressing the spread of female torsos only around the hips, belly and buttocks, all formerly augmented by big skirts. This left ribs unfettered and breasts free to sink. It very noticeably abandoned the old structure that had anchored the female figure and its clothes around a very narrow waist and rib-cage, with bosom and pelvis bursting into prominence above and below. The old corset had insisted on the significantly divided feminine shape, with the skirt and its low secrets kept sharply separate from the enticing arrangements above. In the old scheme, there seemed to be no limit to how large either half might become, when each was stopped at the center by the waist's rigid barrier.

Well before the First World War, however, high fashion produced elegant tailored suits for women that skimmed the unified figure from neck to instep, cleared the ground to expose the feet at work, reduced surface ornament to a minimum, and were made in formerly "masculine" fabrics, woolens in dim shades; and I would emphasize that this was an elegant trend, not a practical development. During the war, clothes with military references and a certain severity seemed appropriate, and many women were actually wearing simple civil uniforms of some kind to do the work of absent men. Skirts, which had definitively risen off the ground by 1912, almost reached the knees in 1916, in a spurt of longing that quickly subsided and returned skirts to the ankle until almost ten years later. Surface masculinization was affecting day-

LEFT: R. Howlett, photograph, Isambard Kingdom Brunel against the Chains of the "Great Eastern," English, 1857. BELOW: American photograph, Lincoln with Maj. Gen. McClernan and E. J. Allan Pinkerton near Antietam, 1862.

Realistic suited man. Photography expanded the visual poetry of suits, demonstrating their combined flexibility and stability, remarking on their esthetic scope. Left, the British civil engineer's suit breaks up in a network of wrinkles that form a counterpoint to the chains of his invention, the largest sailing vessel of its time. The American president (below) visits the battlefield in a suit that turns him into a tower, a column, a reassuring and noble monument under the framing tent. For both, a tall hat is the male crown that gives authority, and that also hides possible baldness or anxious furrows on the brow.

RIGHT: Frédéric Bazille, *Portrait of Renoir,*
French, 1867. BELOW: Henri Fantin-
Latour, *Portrait of Manet,* French, 1867.

Artistic suited man. Painters painted each
other in suits, always giving broad expressive possibilities to masculine tailoring. Right, Renoir appears physically
at ease and personally accessible in his
narrow trousers, formal collar and stiff
boots, in a casual portrait that sets off the
painter's vivid face and hands with the
muted abstract shapes of his suit. By contrast, Fantin (below) has rendered Manet
remote and defended by tailoring, his
whiskers a mask and his swagger stick a
barrier, his whole costume more vibrant
than his face. In both, a bright blue necktie offers an imaginative beacon above the
dim black and gray.

ABOVE: Claude Monet, *Bazille and Camille*, French, 1865. RIGHT: John Singer Sargent, *Mr. and Mrs. I. N. Phelps Stokes*, American, 1897.

The French scene shows the lady as a large tame bird majestically trailing her pale plumage across the grass, uninterested in the questioning, reasonable man. Light strikes him; his country suit gives him possession of the park, but not of the rare, mysterious creature in it. Right, the American couple strike the modern note: she sticks out her elbows, smiles confidently, and manages her hat like a cavalier, clad in male neckwear and a feminized version of male tailoring. He stands in her shadow, his white suit eclipsed by her whiter skirt; but his head is above hers, his body stable and calculating, his expression thoughtful. He makes the money, she has the fun.

time fashion, as often before, and as always in wartime; but now the female figure was being whittled down to match the idea.

NEVERTHELESS, in tune with heightened wartime feelings about sex, evening dresses were more gauzy and feminine than ever, now calf-length to show feet and ankles in exciting shoes and stockings, and very loose and revealing above the waist. Without tight waists and big petticoats, the bodies wearing them looked very real indeed, the breasts and hips connected in an organic human relation, and the feet and legs in plain sight. Posture, formerly very straight and queenly to go with the expanse and stiffness of the clothes, now allowed for an easy and relaxed *slouch*—another defining and irreversible sign of female modernity, formerly seen only in advanced works of Pre-Raphaelite art.

But the old customs reassuringly remained, as they still do. Along with the new "reality" of the body, feminine hats became larger than ever since 1780 and more wondrously adorned, and shoes became more erotic and fanciful now that they were always on view. Good sense was visibly remote from the entire enterprise—the soft, free body seemed to require an encumbered head and decorative feet. One can indeed see, from the perspective of distance, that elaborate foot- and headgear were also a feature of the innovative, body-revealing *male* fashions of the late Middle Ages, an added flourish of sexual fantasy in a new climate of male sartorial liberation. Women were finally having their turn in modern times. Throughout this century, we have seen the continuing life of remarkable female shoes, accompanied by extreme hair as well as extreme hats, and elaborate cosmetics. Men had thoroughly explored all these freedoms in the past; women are obviously still not through with them now. And men, of course, have kept the option to take them up again.

Back in this century's second decade, the most important change for women thus occurred when fashion began to demonstrate female sexuality in direct bodily terms, instead of referring to it indirectly. Fashion had recurrently explained the male body in the past, but it had always equivocated and poeticized about the female one. Now women's clothing began to follow the male expository method for the body, but with startling feminine elements. Beginning in about 1913, fashion began to allow female bodies to exercise their direct appeal to the actual sense of

The lady in the photograph plays with masculine formal dress for dashing effect, in elegant daytime wear that is not for riding; her furpiece adds a feminine erotic element. The fashion plate (above) shows the lady pointedly imitating the male silhouette, with a unified outline and simple shapes for hat and suit, both of which are nevertheless distinctly feminine.

touch, as female fashion had never done before, and as male fashion had also never done.

Male dress throughout European history had kept men's bodies intelligible, but it had resolutely prevented them from looking too embraceable or caressable, in order that they not seem vulnerable; and I have claimed that female dress followed that part of the male example, with the addition of contradictory seductive signals. But by 1920, women's clothes not only showed women's structure, they also began to suggest how the female body actually felt to its owner, and how it might feel to the touch of others.

In past fashion, the female appeal to touch had been indirect, with the allure of fabrics making the dress offer itself instead of the occulted and untouchable body. The corsetted waist had invited embrace, but it offered a perverse appeal with refusal built in. Above it, the exposed chest had made the overt claim of smooth sculpture, asking to be seen as part of a work of art to be appreciated from a certain distance; and the woman herself seemed properly distanced from it. In the second decade of this century, however, the furs and soft woolens and silks clinging to the yielding figure seemed at last to confess that a woman could feel her own body; and they straightforwardly invited others to grasp and stroke her as a physically responsive living creature.

Fabrics that slide over the skin give the viewer a strong sense of their surface effect on the wearer. A hemline that cuts directly across the legs at a certain level creates a visible caress of fabric just at that point. The observer can watch the wearer feeling it; and the watcher's hand can sense that it is a mobile, negotiable barrier. Another element in the general effect was the fleshiness still considered appropriate to women, which made their new palpability all the more startling during the wartime and postwar period, before the mode began to demand that women be slim. It might even be said that the generally denuded character of later female fashion came to require the distancing effect of extreme thinness, which in itself tends to repel rather than encourage the reaching hand and embracing arm.

By the twenties and thirties, female designers such as Alix Grès and Madeleine Vionnet were specialists in suggesting the pleasures of touch while maintaining the requisite linear slenderness and aura of refine-

ment. These two used fabric in a sculptural way, as if it were an extension of the mobile flesh, modelling it directly on the body to make a
complete plastic and tangible composition. Gabrielle Chanel, flourishing in the same period, is most famous for making the male suit female
with no hint of androgyny, keeping only its sexual self-confidence and
also insisting on subjective pleasure.

Chanel had begun with easy jersey ensembles and dresses in about
1915, and proceeded to knitted suits and the celebrated Little Black
Dress in the twenties. But it was during the reprise of her career in the
later fifties, in response to the regressive feminine constrictions visible
early in that decade, that Chanel made her famous simple suits in soft
woven woolens with multicolored surfaces. These suits suggested the
kind of erotic self-possession that has no aggression in it, but rather an
element of constant, low-keyed personal bodily delight, a quiet feline
sensuality that is no barrier to active work and thought. The suit for
women—a tailored jacket worn with a skirt, the old riding-habit
scheme—could thus become a costume expressing a purely female sexual independence in the modern world, finally achieved without using
any mannish references, either severe or coy.

Women designers became very important in the profession during
the twenties and thirties, many of them extending the feminine way of
designing to express a subjective, tactile delight in the wearing of clothes,
rather than echoing the standard masculine wish to stun the beholder
with a vision. Masculine designs for women's clothes were influenced
by it, although male designers generally continued, as most still do, to
emphasize the total visual effect, rather than the working beauty of the
garment in wear—to emphasize the apparition, not the organism. Schia-
parelli was one female adherent of the male method, staying always with
purely optical excitement; and some modern versions of the standard
male view could certainly be inspired. Poiret was the first great modern
example, although his career foundered in the twenties; Balmain, Dior
and Balenciaga continued the dazzling Worth tradition, as Givenchy still
does and Lacroix wishes to do. The exceptions to the rule have been
justly celebrated: Patou and Molyneux in the past, Yves Saint Laurent in
more recent days. Giorgio Armani and several other non-Frenchmen
have lately shown the influence of the mobile and tactile ideal that was

originally a female contribution to modern clothing design. Women such as Norma Kamali and Donna Karan are keeping it up.

The famous "comfort" in all of this, I would insist, was not fundamentally a matter of practical convenience for women, nor of grateful liberation from corsets. The point was not to be able to do more physically taxing things—women had done those in all sorts of clothing for centuries, without much honor. It instead concerned a new style of female corporeal pleasure, one more visibly expressive of what women had always liked about their own bodies, the physical feel of flexibility and articulation in both limbs and torso even without vigorous activity, the sense of subtle muscular movement and the strength of bones under smooth skin, the rhythmic shift of weight. Literature and nude art show that men had always admired women's bodies for these very qualities; but during most of European history they were personal secrets, only to be privately enjoyed and perhaps revealed by artists, but never openly expressed by fashion itself.

Only men's clothing, with suits being the last version, expressed the idea of a man's body as a visibly working, self-aware and unified instrument. And twentieth-century men's suits, it may be noted, also seem to touch all of the body's surface with mobile fabric, in a caress that can be watched as it is felt. In keeping with male requirements, however, they can also look properly invulnerable, depending on behavior and circumstances.

IN THIS CENTURY, the erotic force of female bodily movement and bodily surface, and of clothes that not only showed them but emphasized them, were at last publicly acknowledged by fashion. Formerly, constriction, concealment and decorative projection had in fact been "comfortable," because they had been esthetically, socially, and above all sexually satisfying, despite the noise people sometimes made against them. They became really insupportable only as the social agreements and sexual fantasies of men and women changed their terms.

The changes in women's fashion coincided with the spread of close couple-dancing as an ordinary pastime, and of movies showing ideal male and female bodies engaging in all sorts of action inside their mobile garments, grasping and touching each other in new styles of movement that matched the clothes. In such visions, the masculine suit held its own as a perfect envelope for exuberant modern motion. We can see it in the fine visual harmony created by smooth Vernon Castle and fleet Fred Astaire in their endlessly fluent tailoring.

The change in the sexual agreement between men and women was mainly enabled by changes in female image and self-image; and these, too, were embodied in the new views of women projected by Hollywood, which offered a succession of new parts for women to play. Until this century, and until the movies, the ideal well-dressed woman had been the Lady, a cultivated personage whose mature style and charm had been carefully developed over time, with the support of the social position and income of her father and her husband. The counter-image was the Courtesan, equally schooled and seasoned, often equally refined, supported by the same men. Young girls might be potential Courtesans or Ladies, but from the fashionable point of view, their figures and conversation had only a raw, awkward charm and no style at all, and their lives no scope. They lacked training, experience, and fully developed bodies; elegance was not at all suitable to them.

The modern elegant woman, by contrast, ceased being a mature Woman and became an independent Girl, in a variety of styles. Hollywood first showed her in a divided image roughly describable as the Vamp and the Child, Theda Bara and Mary Pickford, both caricatures. These extreme American visions were nevertheless clearly echoed in the work of French designers such as Poiret, who offered both smouldering adventuresses in heavy satin drapes and egrets, and guileless creatures in sweet sailor hats and pleated linen skirts. Later came the Madcap Heiress, an uneasy blend of child and vamp. All of this went on before 1925, as society struggled with new conceptions of female freedom and female sexuality, both of which still seemed to be publicly forbidden, uncontrollable things: harlots and infants are known to be very dangerous objects of desire.

The synthesis appeared in the next few years in the Hollywood image of Clara Bow, the sexy but self-respecting and humorous Young Girl who makes her own legitimate way, wearing bright, crisp, mobile garments that show her using her legs, both to dance with pleasure and to stride ahead with purpose. Many cinematic versions of her helped create a new ideal woman, and a new modern elegance that displayed no need either for the cumulative effects of experience nor the results of detailed maintenance. The sophisticated French version of this American image was the actual figure of Chanel herself, who showed how to be a young, slim and independent Girl until she died at the age of eighty-eight, still addressed as "Mademoiselle." She was the lover of many but nobody's wife, mother or daughter, rich by her own professional efforts, a good friend and social equal of the great and near-great. It was all unheard of before, except for notorious stage performers beyond the social pale. But twentieth-century society recognized such a person as respectable. Her clothes—elegant, sexy and youthful all at the same time—now had to reflect both her modern freedom and her essential honor.

STAYS

A FINAL WORD about those tight corsets and long petticoats. Even though our present period elevates rebelliousness as a natural and universal feeling, even a virtue, it should not be assumed that all the women in the past were angry victims in their long skirts and tight stays, and felt forced into helplessness because of them. Elizabeth I, Catherine de' Medici and Catherine the Great were heads of state who steered their nations through difficult times with great political talent, energy and application, usually dressed in garments of great weight and stiffness that were tightly constricted in the mid-section and had skirts and sleeves of immense size. For those women, there is no question that their own sense of authority, and even of political and intellectual *agility*, was enhanced and supported by those clothes. The costume also added the dimension of female sexual force to the effect produced on the wearer's own self and on others. Elizabeth was always thin, but the two different Catherines became very heavy in later life. The sheer size of them fully dressed in royal gear was obviously immensely effective, perhaps more so than male equivalents at the time.

Such clothing certainly did not confine those queens to the sofa, nor their conversation to frivolities, nor did it perpetually encourage them to faint, nor to feel submissive and inactive. Nor, I would say, to feel uncomfortable. In fact, both the inward feeling and the outward aspect of persons in their situation, male or female, who preserve bodily decorum, mental energy and rhetorical skill, who maintain good temper and good manners along with the capacity to stand, sit and walk with majestic ease and to ride horseback and dance gracefully for hours, all while visibly transcending the constant challenge of such garments, are infused with the aura of power and triumph, not with the sense of submission to burdens. Men and women both engaged in producing such effects.

The place where we can now see how it all used to work is on the operatic stage. The male and female stars of Verdi's *Don Carlos,* for example, which is set in the period of Elizabeth I and Catherine de' Medici, wear costumes that are just as rigid, heavy and extensive as the Renaissance ones were, and just as laden with surface incrustations, stiff ruffs, fancy hats and elaborate underpinnings. These performers can be observed singing difficult music with sensitive artistry, acting vivid drama with sustained conviction, marching or standing, bowing or kneeling with unfailing dignity and dancing in perfect rhythm, all while keeping their eye on the conductor, remembering the notes, text and blocking, keeping control of their delicate vocal instrument and managing all that glittering weight, stiffness and yardage as if it were nothing. Such achievements by both men and women are enthusiastically and justly applauded by modern spectators, and not just for the beauty of tonal production. Modern audiences, committed to an ideal of stripped-down flexible coverings, may well feel a trace of envy and wonder.

In Renaissance real life, the nobility and gentry of both sexes participated in such sartorial heroism as they still did in Catherine the Great's time, and indeed in the nineteenth century, when not only feminine skirts but military dress uniform reached extremes of rigidity and display. Masculine corsetting, then frequently undertaken to preserve the stiff perfection of formal military costume, had in fact a history going back to the strict girding of fighting men's loins in ancient cultures. The wearing of stays, whether they were sewn directly into the clothes or worn in a separate corset, was undertaken by both men and women with an awareness of the serious inner and outer power it conferred, erotic power not the least, which transcended any trivial bodily inconvenience. We have already mentioned the attractions of visible sexual heroism, the breathtaking, seductive look of effortless effort.

In an echo of this, and in the same way, generations of ordinary women in their long skirts and stiff bodices could feel supported and enabled by them, fully armed and well presented, attractive and considerable both as women and as persons, their secrets intact. They might also feel sober or sexy in them, energetic or languid, or all of these, depending only on personality and milieu.

Ordinary physical activity was manifestly not impeded by such clothing, including the rather athletic dancing of the past, and there are photographs of mountain climbers in multiple skirts, along with tennis-players and ice skaters. Generations of laced-up, long-skirted women went up and down stairs all day doing household tasks, bending over washtubs, beating carpets, reaching up to clotheslines and running after children. Ordinary farm labor was undertaken in stays and long skirts, as illustrated in Van Gogh and Millet paintings, for example, and certainly by factory workers and city workers in all white-collar jobs, as texts and pictures show. In cities, it was thought that only whores with loose morals or slatterns with slack habits went around without stays. Undoubtedly there were field-laborers and mine-workers who also did not wear them; but the custom was standard in all classes. Idle wives, giddy girls and dissipated courtesans undoubtedly wore them, too; and many in all categories may well have felt constrained by the costume.

But overwhelming evidence suggests that this normal female gear provided deep general satisfaction for centuries. It gave women the sense of completeness that acceptable clothing always gives, which is its true comfort. Such comfort is an inward satisfaction, and obtains even in solitude; it does not require social or sexual display to have its effect. Plenty of women regularly wore tight stays and full petticoats with the personal sense of being comfortably dressed, with no thought of receiving company or leaving the house or pleasing a man, as a modern woman might wear a loose sweater and tight bluejeans.

Extreme tight-lacing, so famously barbaric, was always a very rare custom, a fetish first practiced in the sixteenth century and reaching its height in the later nineteenth, just when all feminine trappings were beginning to seem oppressive. Fetishistic tight-lacing—which could involve gradual diminution of the waist down to the neighborhood of fourteen inches—was never common, either among upper-class women or ordinary middle-class ones. It was usually found among working city girls, the same people who now might regularly wear two-inch fingernails and four-inch high heels. The famous evidence for dislodged bones and organs was found in work-house corpses, not among the petted ladies of the upper bourgeoisie—although some anxious middle-class young girls seem to have taken up extreme tight-lacing the way some modern ones take up starving. Fainting was apparently a female response possible under all circumstances without the need of stays, usually caused by a mixture of physical and mental stress not connected with constriction.

Most corsetting simply gave a neat line to the figure, and supported the correct fit of the bodice and the right hang of the skirt rather than primarily imposing an unbearable grip around the body. The grip was firm, rather; and since it produced both elegance and countenance, it was often more reassuring than troublesome, in the days before muscle-training was fashionable. By suggesting a certain self-respect, it had a protective character. In the erotic mode, it provided a dynamic difference between the sleek dressed figure and the soft nude body. For the four centuries before the later nineteenth, in other words, women seem to have had no trouble feeling real in their stays and long skirts.

In general, people have always worn what they wanted to wear; fashion exists to keep fulfilling that desire. But since fashion is committed to perpetual contingency, and anything chic has only a provisional dominance, however strong, protests against accepted modes have always been a present feature in the common life of fashion. They appeal to people's underlying knowledge that fashion is irrational. Fashionable peculiarities even seem purposely designed to attract objections, and they always make an easy target for any individual rebel or determined rhetorician. But only a deep and general discontent provides the vital impulse to replace them with the next fashion, as we have determined. Although many, many girls doubtless rebelled against stays ever since the sixteenth century—or varieties of long skirt, or hair-curling devices— most of them must have come to feel the satisfaction in them, since stays and long skirts and curls didn't vanish. For most women, they clearly offered many more positive pleasures than constant martyrdom. Not only male but female sexual fantasy was bound up with them; they answered to a broad range of imaginative needs.

But only until this century, when a new range came into existence, and the old trappings ceased to satisfy. They had in fact, as we have seen, been showing their failings rather than their virtues for some time before, and complaints were becoming general rather than isolated and individual, or partisan and political. The modern changes had the flavor of instant liberation when they were finally complete, as if an unexpected battle had suddenly been quickly won—people like to say the First World War was responsible. The new changes were actually the end of a long process of modification that proved irreversible because of its very evolutionary character. The modern sartorial transformation of women took a long time; and although the social changes of the same period were immense, it was the sexual and esthetic ones that began the real differences in female shape, line, form and texture.

REDESIGNING WOMEN

FEMALE IMAGINATIVE influence was certainly not the only thing that brought about change in women's appearance in the first third of this century. More than anything else, the new possibility of good ready-to-wear clothing and elegant mass-produced fashion for women contributed, as it had done for male dress a hundred years earlier, to a modernization of desirable female looks. The change again visibly levelled the old primitive sort of class distinction, and with that some of the most noticeable old gender distinctions. As it had long since done for men, good-looking ready-made clothing for women became available in department stores and even by mail-order in the last two decades of the nineteenth century. Most of it was offered in the simplified tailored style that was already modish at the highest level—the easy sort of clothing that does not necessarily require perfect custom fitting.

In the 1890's, hard-working secretaries and shop-assistants in New York or London could already buy neat ready-made suits and feel well turned out, just as their brothers and husbands did, in clothes that had their own modern virtue and did not look like botched attempts at higher elegance. Extremely various and beautifully trimmed ready-to-wear shirtwaists were also a feature of the turn-of-the-century working-girl's looks, a becoming and distinctive mode quite remote from made-to-order high fashion.

The real modernization of fashion depended on a rise in the status of mass-produced machine-made garments, accompanying the rise in the esthetic status of all industrial design. "Design" had long been an elevated activity, the proper concern of a truly creative spirit. But that idea had presumed a craft tradition in which the designed object is an individual masterpiece, a Paul Revere teapot or a Cellini cup. Dressmakers and tailors had participated in the tradition, although at a much lower level—their names only became generally celebrated in the nineteenth century, among the nouveau-riche status-seekers of the period. At that time, however, machine-made objects had very low status, and the great defenders of beautifully designed things, Ruskin and William Morris and others, firmly opposed them to anything a soulless factory might make its hapless workers produce by machine.

In this century, a continuing admiration for the imposing technical achievements of the last one, with its Eiffel Tower, its trains, steamships and suspension bridges, was extended to embrace technical achievements of mobile and portable and commonly available kinds, airplanes and automobiles, telephones and coffee-pots. The designers of such things were inspired to display as much respect as any traditional craftsmen for basic materials and primary function; and the public was encouraged to love well-designed industrial products for their sleek beauty, and to buy them in great numbers. Their availability and cheapness were virtues that could only enhance their intrinsic good looks, now dependent on the newly dynamic and sexually charged look of practical function.

With love came respect for the infinite reproducibility of such objects, the delicious knowledge that each example is automatically made to the same high standard of technical perfection. A new esthetic based on the ideal of perfect alikeness could replace, or certainly rival, the old one of individual uniqueness. Standard sizing for light-bulb necks, plugs and lampshades, bedsprings and bed-linens, bottlecaps and many other objects aided in the gratification of the public's sensual pleasure in multiple industrially made goods, with everything wonderfully made to connect with everything else. Graduated standard sizing eventually extended to stockings and brassières, blouses and skirts, shoes and gloves. The beauty of such things lies in their very aptness for being identically multiplied, their wonderfully machine-cut, machine-stitched, unfailing perfection. Jeans offer the best present-day example of delicious factory-made looks; and like them, the development I have described was largely an American phenomenon. French modern design was still mostly a matter of exquisite individual conception and craftsmanship, and most French modern fashion was still made to order.

American modernization allowed women's clothing to participate equally with men's in the new impersonal character of American modern design itself. When a designer's original idea can easily be adapted to mass production and can become familiar to many people in many different contexts, it quickly loses the look of an individual invention. For American women, modernization could neatly include the transformation of the Clothed Woman as Designed Object into something with a share in the excitement generated by modern architecture and industrial manufacture, something the whole temper of society seemed to be creating. A woman could seem like a sleek new streamlined machine, that universal object of longing, instead of fashion's doll or singular fetish; and she could seem self-created. Just as with all other objects, a vast array of available mass-produced garments puts the main creative emphasis on the choices of the consumer, and removes it from those of the original designers. At the present moment, the Gap clothing company advertises its wares as neutral objects entirely at the disposal of imaginative individual customers; not a word about the clever people who actually design the clothes.

As it had done with men's tailoring, democratization thus worked its way unnoticeably into feminine fashion. Haute Couture garments were becoming unostentatious and simple; and at the same time, inexpensive mass-produced garments could be worn as excellent examples of chic modern design, with no hint of snobbish self-consciousness about the poor unsuccessfully aping the rich, or the rich condescendingly aping the poor. From a certain distance on the city street, individual feminine taste could make a much more noticeable difference than riches or poverty did, just as with male dress. By the 1920's, the ready-to-wear *look* had affected the Haute Couture itself, and a certain abstract generality overtook the desirable clothed appearance for women, even at the couture level. This look had a striking similarity with the long-standing desirable looks for men—reduced, abstract, and similar.

After a long period of slow reform, the final stage did take a very short time. Between 1920 and 1930, ordinary women's clothed bodies were entirely transformed to suggest sexual equality with men. In general this carried no sense of sexual similarity or identity; but a singular feature did arise in feminine fashion—boyishness made its appearance. With the new reduced scope of female clothing, the smaller size of women became more evident. In order to keep women looking free and not dependent, fashion provisionally allowed them to resemble dashing youths or cheeky urchins.

Up to the end of the thirties, however, the skirt was still universal in fashion, with trousers a rare anomaly, always a special case. Trousers had appeared as early as 1911, not for sport or convenience but as an advanced and outré possibility in the Haute Couture, and women had worn knickers for cycling before that; but pants still remained marginal and unusual, sometimes part of upper-class sportswear, sometimes part of another old upper-class impulse to stress androgyny in erotic ways. But fashion for women in general remained traditionally feminine, quite recognizable if radically modified. Women kept the privilege of using ornament and color according to expressive inclination; but these were now deployed in a reduced formal scheme that held the element of fantasy to the same integrating rules of design governing all other man-made things.

Before the articulating but concealing male trouser could possibly be accepted as normal female dress, women's legs needed time to become a customary sight, especially to women themselves. The female leg had to seem as common and various as the female face and hands, and just as active in everyday life. Pants had to wait until legs were old news; and the revelation by fashion that the lower half of the female body had a constant and necessary relation to the upper half took the best part of this century to get used to. The permanent shortening of skirts was the most necessary step in furthering the modernization of women, the most original modern contribution to feminine fashion accomplished without recourse to the standard male vocabulary. It was a crucial modern move in the ancient feminine game of selective exposure.

The short and narrow skirt was visually far more radical than any other modern change, except for the shift to tactile emphasis; it finally gave the female body a coherence that had been a male privilege—the head was shown to have a necessary relation to the feet, as thought has to action. Incidentally, even short skirts could represent an obscure acknowledgment of masculine sartorial superiority—one might see it as still another late female reprise of the fourteenth-century male revolution, when men first began to articulate the male body by displaying the full scope of its legs, while leaving women's under wraps. Women in the modern world finally took up the option of the variable hemline, an effect used in men's tunics for three centuries before breeches definitively took over in the sixteenth century.

Fashion had briefly attempted hem-shortening for women a few times before—in the 1770's, again in about 1830, and briefly in the late 1860's—but always with a skirt that formed a stiff bell and kept the daring feet and ankles from any connection with the rest of the body. Skirts soon sank down again each time, after exposing female feet as apparently detachable ornaments. Since long skirts had commonly distorted female visual proportions for centuries, while male clothes honored male ones, the first function of small, short modern skirts was to put women's clothed bodies into a complete physical correspondence with men's. Nude art had given it to them, but never fashion; and now clothed parity was achieved and kept. It established the visual assumption of public equality for men and women, the image of a steady desire.

By 1925, modern skirts were knee-length and not cumbersome, and they gave off no mysterious suggestions. After that, the hem moved up and down, but never all the way down for good. Skirts tended to delineate the pelvis and thighs, to move with them instead of independently, and to cover the form with what seemed like a single layer of fabric, just as men's trousers did. If skirts in the twenties and thirties ever stuck out or dragged on the ground, they did it for occasional pleasure and not on principle. Modern hats became creatively feminine, taking inventive and suggestive shapes around the shape of the head, rather than following ancient male formulas. They forswore any vestige of the old female coif or bonnet, and they also stopped trying to carry the whole burden of past frivolities. Attached to them, modern veils were ornamental, small and seductive with no trace of modesty.

Thus, although still so different in character, the modern clothed bodies of men and women were visibly made on the same human scale and had equally functional legs and feet, their hats were of similar size, and their hair took up about the same amount of space. Similar bathing suits began to display their limbs and torsos in equally active motion. Only female shoes kept the ancient shared adherence to fetishism and difficulty; and a new distinctively female revival of ancient shared custom was the vivid use of makeup. The elements of adult female fashion that are still the basis of modern clothing for women—the smooth-fitting tailored jackets and skirts, the tailored slacks, the deftly shaped dresses, the soft sweaters and flattering blouses ranging from tailored shirt to frilled or draped confection—were established in the 1920's and 1930's, after realistic feminine proportions had been acknowledged and the female clothed body was given its own dignified visual unity for the first time since antiquity.

The entire scheme was then seen as immensely radical and definitively liberating; and so it has proved, although a considerable regression took place during and after the Second World War. Because of the return to a certain Victorian style for women's clothes and lives, the decade of the 1950's has lately seemed to have eradicated the triumphant revolution achieved at the beginning of the century, and to blend in people's minds with the Victorian era itself. The 1940's began this return from advanced modernism, with a new fragmentation of ornament, a new fussiness or grotesquerie to the general female outline, partly inspired by another war.

The early fifties produced a more esthetically integrated style, but with the old constrictions revived—although just as with the famous twenties, the modes of about five years have loomed very large in remembrance. Many now believe that there was no freedom at all in female clothing before 1968, as if that revolution, by rebelling against the fifties, produced a single sartorial liberation of the female sex, imprisoned since the Middle Ages. But such an assumption betrays the more important and lasting changes of form gradually accomplished in the four decades before 1940—during which time huge numbers of modern women acquired respectable educations and serious careers, the vote, and the benefits of effective contraception, even without gaining the universal respect that would properly match such developments.

During that long period, female fashion not only allowed flexibility and touchability to the whole body, but for the first time considered the fact that breasts, because they are linked to the muscles of the chest and arms but have none of their own, constantly shift shape and position and tend ultimately to sag. The modern brassière, perfected in the 1930's, was designed to let breasts of all sizes move with the body, to hold them protectively in smooth pockets without pressing them up or in, as stiff corsets had done, but also without letting them sink.

Nevertheless the modern bra could be used to push breasts around even more than corsets had, and early versions suppressed them, both to favor the new abstract unity of the body and to enhance the modish look of unripe youth. Later on in the America of the forties and fifties, it was clear that although big breasts had become more desirable than ever, their ordinary behavior had again become an inadmissible fact. Movie actresses would ride horseback or run downstairs with unbelievably static mammary projections fixed high on their chests, which looked especially ridiculous if the costume was a nightgown or an ancient Greek tunic.

In the revolutionary late sixties, bras thus acquired temporary associations with falsity and prurience, just as if they were new versions of old corsets. But when mobile breasts and visible nipples reappeared in fashion and bras became permissibly absent, objections to them quickly vanished in the face of women's increasing claim to have their individual fantasies taken seriously by fashion. Women reclaimed the right to wear supportive or constrictive underwear if they chose, but not if they didn't; and bras became just like skirts, optional elements subject to all kinds of fashionable variation and connotation. Lately the accumulated imagery of the feminine has finally been delivered up to women to do what they liked with, to rifle as if it were a costume trunk—they can use all of it, just as they have used all male imagery.

It was a signal early triumph, however, that the modernizing impulse in female fashion right away acknowledged that not all women have sizeable, hemispherical, and very firm breasts set high on the rib-cage— blurring of the mammary outlines had already occurred soon after 1900. The mode of the twenties seemed to be finally celebrating an absolute freedom from the famous high roundness of breasts, a primary reference of female fashion for such a very long time. Flat-chested women had their first great day of recognition in the modern world. Not only that, female waists and hips were at last perceived to come in varying sizes and at varying levels. Scrawny and shapeless women also came into their own, and an unclear waistline and narrow hips became female character-istics acknowledged by fashion, right along with the small breasts, a flat behind, and a highly visible bone-structure.

The male suit had been allowing for bodily variation all along, easily flattering all shapes with its flexible scheme. Women's classic modern fashion now did the same; and indeed it was only with this new mod-ernization that "classics" could begin to exist in female fashion. Classi-cism in fashion required modernity of form, a basic and variable formal language that could offer more freedom in design, not less—an escape out of time-bound, quickly dated surface trivia and into the world of strong and important formal ideas.

Fashion also came visibly to admit that female hair might be of vary-ing thickness and sparseness, so that it might sometimes look better when short and loose instead of always trying to seem long and heavy, as female hair had forever been supposed to be. Hair was made free of the need for careful coiling and braiding and curling, and artificial help if it wasn't abundant. Sexual assertion through hair became licensed for women—they could swing it and toss it and show off its vitality, as men had done, instead of publicly carrying it around like an extra female body, beautiful and wayward and in perpetual need of strict regulation.

By creating a new kind of variability for female physical appearance, which was not an imitation of but an analogue to the one in men's clothes, fashion now expressed the idea that men and women are equal in their capacity to be complicated human individuals, each visibly pos-sessing a unique private character, mental furniture and inner life. We have seen how abstract simplicity and similarity in the forms of dress, in the modern male mode, serve to emphasize truly individual personal traits. Personal beauty, considered a female obligation, also became a variable individual matter no longer associated only with a perfect young face and figure.

The increasingly profitable cosmetics industry emphasized this new modern fact, encouraging the gathering of rosebuds throughout life, not just in adolescence. Just as bodies of all sorts could be flattered by modern fashion, faces of all sorts could be enhanced with makeup. Makeup became the emblem of the conscious, creative charm that transcends all indifferent physical attributes, and therefore makes age irrelevant. Helena Rubinstein, the cosmetics tycoon, is alleged to have said, "There are no ugly women, only lazy ones."

Meanwhile mobility and palpability, replacing stasis and inviolability, became the desirable attributes of the clothed female body, not just of its garments or of its secret nude state. A visible integration took place between the entire living, sentient woman and her costume. Like her male counterpart, she, too, could now suggest the self-possessed animal happy in its skin. As a material phenomenon, an elegantly clothed woman thus ceased to be like a tree or a house, rooted, sheltering and decked out, or like a lifeless doll animated only by ornament, still less like a decorated balloon or full-rigged ship at the mercy of the capricious wind, and much more like a self-propelled car or motorboat, smoothly designed, vibrating with life, built and fitted for graceful speed.

MODERN TRANSFORMATIONS

WE HAVE SEEN how masculine costume during this same period, without actually changing much, came to suggest the same things. Since masculine suits had been in the vanguard of the modern esthetic impulse anyway, they already had the ability to suggest anything advanced. In their prophetic modern classicism, they had been evolving uninterruptedly toward further modernity during the whole nineteenth century, even while the general visual character of both the fine and applied arts had veered back toward a revived Rococo spirit or a Romantic historicism. Women's costume had gone that way, too, in keeping with the idea of Woman as both ornamental and unaccountable.

Victorian dress for elegant men had certainly included many opportunities for fashionable discomfort and conspicuous consumption. But the forms themselves had remained simple, and men were always visibly straightforward, their clothes candid reflections of male interest in the concerted advance of thought, science and commerce, and lack of concern for capricious and suggestive trifles of any sort—what have been called bourgeois values. Paintings of the later nineteenth century often contrast a somber-suited man with the riotous light, motion, and color of the natural world. Such works figure man's moral and intellectual superiority to the brilliant lack of discipline in nature, while at the same time suggesting the strong appeal of its beauty and volatility. His suit was not supposed to be beautiful, but reasonable by contrast—there had been a change since the buff and dun colors of men's tailored clothes had seemed to blend with fields and forests.

Romantic visions reinforced the assumption that Nature is female, exempt from carrying the heavy burden of human understanding that was perceived as essentially male. But male conscious will longed to master what it saw to be the mercurial, mysterious and powerful beauty of the Natural, now conflated with the Feminine, some of which manifests itself inwardly in the spiritual and instinctive life of either sex. Men, by taking women to be embodiments of Nature, could even cherish the equivocal belief that Nature herself longs to be understood and put into intelligible order by Man, "created" by him in a formally manageable shape, so that his conscious reverence for it and pleasure in it may mask his unconscious dread of its force.

That general state of double longing is what fashion for the two sexes was then illustrating. Along with the beauty of the external natural world—flowers, water, clouds, stars—women's dress also suggested the natural inner world, the flow of dream, fear and unexpressed wish. Men could feel pleasure at seeing women clad in well-composed toilettes that visibly tamed the forces they invoked. Women could be pleased to contemplate men dressed in their reassuringly endless expressions of desire for order and sanity. Double portraits, like two-sexed fashion plates and genre scenes of the Victorian period, opposed vivid female fantasy to sober male clarity, frequently in an outdoor setting.

In the early part of this century, comprehensive stability lost a lot of ground as the primary male sartorial theme. Not the design but the multiplicity of male elegance was reduced in scope; and between 1910 and 1930, male lounge-suits came into their own as esthetic echoes of the machine age. The same smooth tubes of sleeve and trouser and the neat shapes of collar and tie now came to look functional and streamlined instead of infinitely masterful and trustworthy, or daringly revolutionary as they had done when they first appeared. Works of art and fashion art came to harmonize them with similarly sleek and tubular women and with equally trim buildings. We can see how the allegedly "phallic" look of narrow, smooth, fast-moving objects became a formal element of neutral erotic power without specifically male or female associations.

All of nature itself soon came to submit to the same abstraction of visual form, following the new rules of modern art. Nature no longer seemed so much at odds with tailoring, which therefore came again to seem more natural, just as in Neo-classic times. Visual life soon made a claim on the emerging sense of physical truth as consisting of fundamental structures that can be known and understood, or of fundamental conceptions that can be diagrammed. Mystery was no longer attractive. Nature, human nature and culture were being submitted to the same modern intellectual rules, and all man-made objects were being designed to suggest an acknowledgment of structural dynamics. The two sexes thus found a new basis on which to design their visual equality.

Images in paintings as well as in popular art and fashion art now showed how formerly opposed things could submit to a new unity of graphic understanding. According to modern rules for the abstraction of form, clothed men and women were as naturally similar as nude ones, and both were similar to hills and buildings, as all came under the detached creative scrutiny of the modern eye and mind. Women's clothes had been modified, and women themselves modified, partly to conform to this modern idea; but it is noticeable that the actual shapes of men's suits did not have to be changed, only the sense of what they expressed. The form was already there, and held its own appeal, which was now perceived to come from new sources. Modern abstract form was not static but dynamic: modern suits could cease to seem unredeemably firm and grim, carefully opposed to the fluid, giddy whirl of nature, or of feminine dress. Instead, they could share in the joyful new vibrancy of solidly designed and constructed modern views and modern visions, visibly humming with potential action and inner energy, just like modern nature.

Female garments, like male ones, now showed how they were constructed, with undisguised seaming and piecing. The basic character of the cloth was respected, not vitiated by being cut up into decorative strips, puffs or flaps and then reapplied. Between 1925 and 1935, an ideal feminine ruffle, drape or flounce, for example, would no longer be a small mobile detail, catching attention on the surface of a stable shape, but the integral part of a fluid skirt or sleeve, growing out of it or even creating it. Certainly at the couture level, the beauty of ornament often became identical with the beauty of construction and material. Men and women had visual equality because female dress for the first time was following the masculine example in basic conception, and finally following the superior Neo-classic artistic example of copying methods rather than imitating surface results. The way for women to look as real as men had been perfected, in the context of a universal modern reality for everything. A shared basic structure—atoms and molecules—underlay the entire material world; its image in art and dress could be similarly shared.

The character of fashion for both sexes just before the Second World War was that of an achieved modernity, not unlike what was true of architecture, sculpture, and painting, and the industrial arts. But for fashion, following its representational rule, the look of streamlined function and esthetic integrity was sufficient, and conventional habits were retained within the modernized visual scheme. The new exception was huge visible divisions between the classes. Clothes otherwise kept most old conventions for distinguishing sexes and ages, for preserving social ceremonies, and for keeping old distinctions between underwear and outerwear. Synthetic fibers were not yet well developed, and the traditional fabrics were in traditional use—cotton, silk, linen and wool,

sometimes woven in combination, and supplemented with some artificial silk. All clothes were still troublesome to take care of, as they had always been, and hats were still mandatory for everyone, as some sort of headgear had been for millennia. Continuity was prevailing as usual in fashion, even in the face of radical changes.

During the twenties, in keeping with the right look for everything material during that decade, we have seen how the clothed figures in fashion drawings were designed to resemble hard-edged and streamlined cubes and cylinders, or to look like flat arrangements of geometric pattern. But what is most noticeable about the best of such fashion plates is that for the first time they were being made to echo the style of serious

OPPOSITE: French fashion plate, 1925.
ABOVE: Publicity photograph of Clara Bow, 1928.

The fashion plate now takes note of modern art and graphic design; the woman is seen to be created out of whole cloth, her body and dress stylized into a single modern shape. The movie star's image gives the same message by camera means: her body is molded into a sheath of fluid light by the colorless satin. Her own physical awareness of the dress against her skin is expressed in her sinuous pose and self-conscious gaze.

LEFT: Snapshot of Marlene Dietrich, 1932.
BELOW: Man Ray, *Portrait of Balthus*, 1933.
OPPOSITE: Esther Bubley, *Greyhound Bus Terminal, New York City*, 1948.

The camera continues to enhance the modern beauty of suits in wear, showing how they flatter bodily motion, making art out of the casual action of sleeves and trousers. Individual faces take on more prominence as they rise above the scheme of folds that describes the body's easy pose. Dietrich often used male dress to enrich the look of her suggestive face; here the neutral beret and sweater redeem her suit from pure transvestism.

modern painters. There are wonderful fashion illustrations that seem to turn the modish figure into part of a Braque or a Léger, or into a personage from a Maurice Denis dream-world. Accompanying such images were small bits of fashion copy that imitated the suggestive phrases of modern poetry and fiction, instead of resorting to the straightforward or inanely coy descriptions used in Victorian fashion plates.

The images in Victorian fashion plates were in fact debased versions of much older forms of art, invoking the flattering conventions for rendering dress that had prevailed in the genre-painting and portraiture of past centuries. During those centuries, even the most bizarre fashion had been given an air of natural nobility and perfection by Bronzino and Titian, Van Dyck and Terborch, Gainsborough and Boucher. Fashion art by the middle of the nineteenth century was attempting to recover some of that idealizing spirit, but with no artistic convictions and consequently with very indifferent results. Better by far are the first true fashion plates at the end of the eighteenth century and those in the early nineteenth, which are brilliant examples of purely graphic art with no apologies to painting, and with a keen sense of the verve and quirky impact of fashion.

Looking back, it is remarkable that during the great flowering of French art that produced Monet's *Women in the Garden,* with its blend of delicious dresses, grasses and flowers creating a new world of painted glitter that gives fashion great importance, the actual art of fashion illustration was banal and retrograde in the extreme. None of its practitioners attempted to suggest the developments in the artistic avant-garde, but rather stayed with decaying academic conventions. In the 1860's, painting was clearly becoming modern, but feminine fashion still was not. Worth and his colleagues were keeping its artistic character wholly literary and illustrative—fictional, as we have said. Fashion art looked like magazine illustration, and neither commanded much public respect. Nor, of course, did fashion.

It is therefore important that fashion illustration once again became an immensely advanced graphic vehicle during the first three decades of this century, by comparison to its character in the later nineteenth. It came to share in the new respect for graphic design, which was a serious part of design in general. Respect for coherent and vivid compositions was extended to theater sets and book illustration, and fashion art was included among such enterprises. These all gained a prestige that helped raise the esthetic prestige of fashion itself.

The new seriousness of fashion went with the new reality of women; but even more than that, an idea was beginning to arise that all dress is serious, whatever form it takes. The study of anthropology was joined by the new study of psychology, making primitive art look less primitive and far less distant from the visual expressions of modern life. The meaning of these, including those of modern dress, began to show its sources in the newly discovered unconscious, which itself became a modern theme.

In line with such discoveries, photography expanded into unsuspected realms. Photographic Surrealism infused the secret images of fantasy with an unsettling graphic life and truth, developing themes of inner obsession and suppressed anxiety. The modern camera, which had already begun promoting and affecting the perception of modern architecture and sculpture as well as modern machinery, now became supremely important for understanding how clothes were supposed to look.

The sleek abstraction of modern industrial and architectural design had been well conveyed in modern graphic illustration and painting, and the camera could give it the compelling drama of photographic chiaroscuro. But machinery and buildings, however breathtakingly rendered, don't have complicated souls of their own. The fashion camera, creatively following the Surrealist path, came to show how far clothed humans really are from being like any other material things, and to convey how inward and obscure the sources of clothed elegance really are. In response, the forms of clothes began to lose some of their straight clarity and to acquire more troubling nuance: men's suits became more loose-fitting and draped more readily, women's dresses, hats and shoes developed more suggestive shaping and interesting texture.

During the thirties, photography gradually replaced drawing at the highest level of fashion art. Fashion photography developed into a sophisticated medium adopted by the greatest artists of the camera, with a dominant influence on the perception of clothes. The new photographic explorations of inner life in visual terms had demonstrated how vital clothing is to all experience. In harmony with innovative artistic photography, and with the movies and professional photojournalism, fashion plates of the thirties also began to render the fleeting psychological moment for its own brilliant sake. Formerly they had fixed the mode in a static image indebted either to the history of painting and engraving, or to modern decorative art. Now the history of modern fashion instead became permanently wedded to the development of infinitely suggestive camera magic.

This shift of emphasis in fashion imagery had a decisive effect on ideals of dress, and eventually changed the modern character of clothing as well as its looks. Instead of being objects of modern design, intended to look similar to boats and cars, clothed figures in fashion photographs began to look like characters in dreams and daydreams; but more than that, they came to resemble characters in small unfinished film dramas. These had no history and no future, they existed unsettlingly for an instant. Fashion, the very clothes themselves, gradually came to fulfill an ideal not just of swift movement through the action of life, or through the accompanying play of thought and feeling, but an ideal of quick and dramatic replaceability. Mass-produced, filmed moments were to be lived through, clad in a shifting sequence of mass-produced garments, each ensemble giving way to complete new ones. It gradually became an assumption that clothes were not to be remodelled or even radically repaired, only replaced.

The presently huge second-hand clothing business, beginning with the arrival of La Mode Rétro in the 1970's and the subsequent spread of thrift-shop fashion, both real and pretend, was eventually made possible by this modern shift in attitude. Second-hand clothing used to have a very unsavory reputation as something worn only by those too marginal and too degraded to make their own new ones or have them made, something proper to the very poor, what were called the criminal classes. A used-clothing trade had in fact existed over many centuries, mainly dealing in the unpretentious garments worn at the most basic level of society, where someone might sell a coat to buy bread, or earn a few coins so as to buy a coat. The very grand garments of the very rich were also sold to such dealers by servants to whom they had been given, to be bought and refashioned by others for other purposes.

But in one elegant person's wardrobe, although fashion might constantly require new looks, many of these might be created out of existing garments. The precious fabric would be picked apart and recast in a new shape that would retain a strong link to a former life that nourished the new; fashion used to build physically on its own foundations. Even when old assumptions and institutions might be crumbling, clothing itself, with its quasi-organic staying power through quick modish shifts, with its link to its own past in known materials and hand-made structure, could speak to its owners of survival and continuity. In the early part of this century, following the established custom, good fashionable clothes were still often altered to suit next year's shape, and were carefully mended and reconstituted in new ways for their original owners or their families. They might eventually be given away to servants and sometimes to theaters, to be finally worn out or mutilated, with no thought of direct fashionable revival.

But since the huge increase in both attractive mass-produced garments and mass-produced imagery at the same time, fresh used things are much more quickly passed on without any revision at all. At first,

Fashion photograph, dress by Alix Grès, from *Vogue,* 1938.

The photograph renders the classic purity of the dress caught up in an atmospheric drama that invites deeper perception, chiefly of the skill with which the single piece of fabric has been wrought into a modern masterpiece. The beauty of the garment is complete without applied trim or rigid substructure; all embellishment has been created by the controlled manipulation of the material, and only the moving body inside it makes the dress into an intelligible composition. This image represents a high moment in modern feminine fashion, in which the language of masculine tailored simplicity had been thoroughly and fruitfully translated into tactile female terms.

OPPOSITE: Franz Xavier Winterhalter, *Portrait of Empress Elizabeth of Austria*, 1865. BELOW: Horst V. Horst, society photograph, dress by Christian Dior, from *Vogue*, December 1949.

After the Second World War, fashion reverted to Romantic ideals that made an exciting mystery out of female physical being. The tiny pleated bodice of Dior's creation (below), aided by long gloves, permits the elegant head and nude upper body to burst like a flower out of a tight sheath, balanced by the huge bloom of skirt below. The empress's portrait (opposite) shows the source of these effects, with the great spangled cloud of skirt carrying the woman's jewelled head and bust on a corsetted stalk. Both poses emphasize the lady's bare back and shoulders.

Kammerman photograph, Chanel in her apartment, aged seventy-one, 1954.

Chanel always fought the distancing, Romantic view of feminine fashion, both in her first years of success with simple jersey and simple black, and in her later career with simple suits. Her modern ideal of a realistic, corporeally self-possessed female sexuality permitted lifelong attractiveness, of which she was an example herself.

old ideas prevailed, and the new quick turnover consigned many garments to absolute limbo to make way for new ones—the path led in only one direction. Now, however, used garments are repurchased to become fashionable all over again in new contexts, not instantly demoted to the status of non-fashionable junk. With the further help of synthetic fibers that don't wear out, discarded clothes keep their original mass-produced vitality, ready for new action in new dramas, ready to participate directly in further visions without having to die and be reconceived back to life.

THE MODERN IMAGE business, not just the modern clothing business, has been responsible for suggesting the absolutely fleeting character of anything elegant, even something in itself stiff, thick and still. Fashion photographs ever since the thirties have continued to emphasize the dependence of desirable looks on completely ephemeral visual satisfaction, the harmony of the immediate moment only, which exists totally and changes totally, shifting to the next by no visible process. Most of the clothes that make people fit such images are now constructed wholesale by unknown persons, often out of mysteriously made fabrics and also by unseen processes, which can be adjusted to make new sets in great numbers on short notice. Each set is meant to live for a few perfect moments and then be replaced by the next. During the thirties and after, under the influence of the fashion camera but even more of movies, garments ideally began to look not only quickly disposable, but dependent for their beauty on swift changes of ambience and dramatic suggestion. Thus fashion came to seem more and more like a sequence of illustrative costumes—which is the direction in which it has since developed.

Because Greta Garbo and Errol Flynn, or Charlton Heston and Sophia Loren, or Richard Gere and Glenn Close seem exactly the same in modern dress or in romantic costume, in exquisite tailoring and furs or in the dull garments of the working poor, the message has been repeatedly made clear that a modern person, especially of course a woman, with her traditional license for quick emotional change, may keep wholly transforming through clothing, according to mood or occasion, with no loss of personal identity or consistency—and above all without primary consideration of social circumstance.

A post-modern person, now one of either sex, has further learned that not only may disparate wardrobes cohabit in one person's closet, as if on backstage costume racks, but they may now be combined. Beyond the classic cinema, in the new world of music video and free-wheeling, overlapping, unrooted camera imagery, old denim and fresh spangles or pale chiffon and black combat boots are worn not just in quick succession but together. The new freedom of fashion in the last quarter-century has been taken up as a chance not to create new forms, but to play more or less outrageously with all the tough and solid old ones, to unleash a swift stream of imagery bearing a pulsating tide of mixed references.

RECENT REVOLUTIONS

AFTER THE SECOND WORLD WAR, the real power of mass-produced fashion was first fully acknowledged. It was only then that the idea of "tyranny" became firmly associated with the design of fashionable clothing for women. The postwar period was another in which sexual difference was strongly marked in dress, and overtly displaying wayward sexual fantasy in fashion was again very noticeably an exclusively feminine privilege. A return to unmodern circumstances occurred in fashion and in sexual life, as if the great liberating and integrating moves of the teens, twenties and thirties had never occurred. Women wished to reclaim the privileges accorded them in the old romantic fantasies, and at the time they were unwilling to notice the costs. The sexual battles seemed permanently won, like the war; one could forget what the hard struggle had been against, and go back to the pleasures of romance and the dangers of unreality.

Male fashion became more intensely sober, rigid and deliberately reticent, while the feminine fashion business now expanded by promoting and propelling female sexual fantasy back into the vast world of erotic submission and narcissism disguised as modesty, the world of long hair bound up only to be unbound, of tightly girdled waists waiting for male deliverance, of myriad skirts hiding the prizes. Christian Dior was like Worth come to life again, suggesting the unattainable and distracting visions women might wish to become, visions which had to be maintained with a great deal of hidden discipline and effort. The Angel in the House was also revived, and middle-class women again wished to have five children and bake their own bread, instead of becoming brain surgeons or senators as they had thought of doing in the thirties.

But the fashion industry had irreversibly standardized the elements of fashionable dress, and therefore made it more difficult for consumers to manage personal expression in the new romantic style without feeling frustrated, especially on a budget. Personal expression in dress had in fact seriously lost caste, especially in America, where conformity became a stronger impulse than ever. More and more women who didn't feel personally flattered by fashionable trends began to feel threatened by them, even directly attacked by those who created them. Hostility arose especially against the famous male designers, who were becoming glorified and enriched by the renewed power handed to them, and the new publicity accorded them.

Although the couture was still for the few, mass-produced fashions were noticeably derived from it, and these were now available for everyone. Every woman, however, was no longer in a position to alter and rearrange fashionable clothes to suit her own taste and audience; sewing skills were no longer mandatory for all women, and middle-class women no longer had maids who could repair and alter clothing. Ordinary women might feel directly affected by what went on in the elegant workrooms of Paris (or, increasingly, of Milan and New York), but only through the versions offered ready-made in shops. The couture was thus seen as a "dictator," rather than as a wonderfully remote and Parnassian domain of pure elegance, because everyday fashion had become clearly connected to it. Women began to feel a bit helpless, if shops offered nothing they liked, since only some could readily make their own clothes or remake the ready-made ones. If the new styles that swept away the old ones were no more becoming to her, a woman might well feel put upon.

Eventually, resentment against fashion became excessively politicized and associated with the rise and spread of latter-day feminism, among other movements. Women's fashion lost its identification as a collective esthetic medium expressing women's feelings and qualities, but was seen as itself an endemic oppression of them, something generated by a capitalist and patriarchal society to enslave women without their knowing it. The change in the rhetoric about fashion indicated that a new dress-reform movement was clearly due, with clearly named enemies to be vanquished. Reform occurred again in connection with a change in relations between men and women, but now with reference to an industrialized clothing business. Since the sexes were already officially equal, the new method for escaping the romantic myth was to make them seem identical—on the superior masculine model, of course.

The expressive material used for fighting the situation came this time from mass-produced male working clothes, most notably the celebrated bluejeans that took over the second half of this century. These, along with other similar masculine garments such as Army-Navy gear and certain kinds of active sports gear, combined all the virtues of modern design at its mass-produced best with a great apparent absence of erotically divided modishness. The idea that jeans and army fatigues must also be designed, just as gaskets and wall-plugs are designed, was left out of account. Work-clothes looked designed by fiat, and therefore perfect for expressing anti-fashion sentiments on the part of both sexes. Later on, "designer jeans" became a term of fear and scorn when it became clear that somebody is designing everything that's made, and constantly modifying the design for profit motives.

During the Counter-Cultural Revolution, jeans were not the only salient element, but by far the most enduring and potent—mainly because they still participated in the single great masculine tailoring scheme, in its most venerable plebeian version. It was therefore fair game for women in the provocative mode, like all other male clothing, as well as in the new anti-fashion style. Men wishing to scorn suits could wear jeans, too, the way in England during the thirties the same sort of men had defiantly worn corduroys, the earlier uniform of the English working-man. Such sartorial protests could be undertaken without actually abandoning the basic formal scheme, and therefore they could have all the more visual power for looking sane and real, not false or ridiculous.

By comparison, a brief vogue for male robes and gowns failed to survive as a protest against conventional suits. Although ethnic and Eastern elements were introduced into fashion—Latin American, African, Middle Eastern and Asian motifs were effectively added to the general vocabulary of Western fashionable life—these chiefly operated as ornamental features, not basic forms. Hats, shoes, belts and bags, or even vests and shirts for both sexes have recurrently carried the flavors of determined multiculturalism; but the long, enveloping *galabiya* worn daily by Egyptian men, for example, has had little chance of catching on among Western males discontented with formal tailoring. So far, the wrong sexual connotations outweigh the right political ones.

But women, having gradually learned to wear trousers for two generations, could now help themselves to male jeans made with no concessions to female traditions for fastening or cut, and that circumstance felt very liberating at the time. Jeans had been worn by women on farms and ranches for a long while; their advent as female urban fashion had less the look of specifically male dress than the look of unpretentious practical clothing adopted to fight the idea of any fashionable strictures at all. Women came to wear them with tailored jackets just as men did, in a more seriously modern and flexible mode than the most perfect imitation-male pants-suit could offer; but women kept the right to wear them with dressy blouses, elaborate makeup and jewelry. It was only the dreaded skirt that then smacked of slavery. During the crisis of its transformation into optional gear, the modern skirt suffered great abuse which obviously did it no lasting harm whatsoever.

In the 1970's it was already becoming true, however, that a tailored suit all in one fabric for men or women, just like a woman's dress all in one fabric, could come to acquire a constraining flavor by taking on a ceremonial look, the look of the wedding-dress or the parade uniform, even of the religious habit, the look of having a prescribed usage. In some non-ceremonial one-fabric costumes, of course, the opposing look of freedom quickly appeared—the look of the wet-suit, the jump-suit or sweat-suit, the look of the slip or the bathrobe. In fact the modern tailored suit once had that same easy look in the early twentieth century, when it was a lounge-suit; so did modern dresses at the same period, after the complexities of earlier days.

But when women wished once more to take full possession of the tailored idiom in the seventies, they abandoned dresses in favor of "separates," assortments of skirts and jackets of different cuts and fabrics, to be worn with assortments of blouses and sweaters. Trousers could be part of the assortment, too; and women could adjust their looks with great nuance by shifting all the elements around, just as men had always been able to do in the same idiom, only minus the skirts. One-fabric suits for women were only one example of it, and for a time they came to suggest Dressing for Success, rather than the bodily self-possession Chanel had let suits express. The more modern feminine mode has been separate pieces, in another echo of the original male scheme.

A word about sweaters. These were also originally a part of male traditional dress in various cultures, hand-knit warm coverings for shepherds, sailors and fishermen at work outdoors in cold climates. Scottish versions were adapted for fashionable English male sportswear early in this century, and made elegant between the wars by the Prince of Wales, later the Duke of Windsor. Sweaters were thereafter refined and assimilated into all informal tailored schemes for men, sometimes taking the place of waistcoats; and they were in due course taken over by women along with tailoring itself, to become part of the classic female repertoire. But sweaters have always enjoyed greater visual latitude in modern women's fashion than in men's, because their knitted texture has offered varieties of nuance to the modern woman's mobile figure—Chanel was the first to use them for feminine fashion, not female golf clothes. Their rough, lower-class male origins nevertheless combined with their stretching and clinging capacities to keep them pleasantly rakish and daring for women, and these flavors have only enhanced their latter-day, faintly perverse life as elegant garments. So has the sweater's ancient lowly association with warm winter stockings and undergarments.

Lately, sweaters for both sexes have taken on new life in the ever-expanding universe of machine-knit fabrics, many of them of synthetic fiber. This recently discovered world not only creates vividly attractive new streetwear versions for everybody of formerly boring underwear and athletic gear, but permits new kinds of public or private knitted garment to be as light-weight and diaphanous or as tough and elastic as the imagination might wish. Machine-knitting first put sheer stockings within everyone's reach; since then, it has gone on to offer one of the most important spheres for creative present and future fashion, suggesting possibilities for really new basic forms that have yet to appear.

THE CONSTRAINT APPARENTLY connoted by female dresses and male suits at the end of this century has come to include a perceived unacceptable confinement to one sex or another—transvestite games now make fun of this sharp division. We have seen how firmly sexual conventions were upheld in the first half of this century, even while women were experimenting with masculine methods. To make clothing express a more radical form of equality for men and women, something more has lately been needed than simply dressing women in men's suits—that finally smacks too much of giving in to male dominance, unless it is done for fun in the old coquettish form. Women in completely conventional male costume, tuxedos or tailored pants-suits with neckties, still give off the old flavor of feminine provocation, which has its attractions but doesn't at all suggest true parity of the sexes. The real solution has instead been found in dressing everyone like children.

A crowd of adults at a museum or a park now looks just like a school trip. Everyone is in the same colorful zipper jackets, sweaters, pants and shirts worn by kids—which are the same as traditional work-clothes, only made in jolly colors. The custom of putting children in rugged pants, shirts and jackets dates back to the time when men and women still commonly wore suits and dresses for most occasions; but it joins an old Romantic custom of dressing children in exotic or ancient costume, right along with diminutive versions of rough gear, including rough sportswear or military and naval trappings. Sailor suits were among the first of the latter, common on little boys at the turn of the century when parents wore elegant adult finery. Little Roman Soldiers and Pirates or Turks had been around a century before that, and miniature lumberjacks and railroad men came in this century. But by that time, putting children into tough play-clothes had begun to look enlightened rather than romantic, something done for their good, not for their parents' amusement.

The one-color jump-suits and sweat-suits made for adults, along with bright-colored little gym shorts and tee-shirts, now suggest the rompers and playsuits once worn by infants of both sexes. They are costumes connoting absolute bodily freedom and no responsibilities outside the self, with no need to live up to the original function of the garment. Further, the entire dimension of historic-cum-theatrical costume that has invaded mainstream fashion looks like an adult adaptation from the former privileges of carefree children. It was this freedom from responsibility that parents were emphasizing when they costumed their children in garb that had been highly menacing in its original form, but that clearly denoted harmless play when sported by innocents under ten.

Such clothing moreover strongly connotes freedom from the burdens of adult sexuality. This last seems the most pronounced theme underlying the tendency for men and women to dress exactly alike in versions of sand-box gear, or parody-hunting or parody-laboring gear. Since the middle of this century, little boys and girls have been put into identical masculine play-clothes, at an age when their clothes need not differentiate the sexes because their activities are not supposed to, and neither are their thoughts. Men and women in infant's wear may appear to be claiming that the strategies of the mating game never enter their minds; sex will have to take them unawares. Meanwhile a reverse style of romanticism about children can occasionally result in a mother, wearing jeans, boots and a windbreaker, walking hand in hand with a little girl wearing a bouffant velvet dress with a lace collar and dainty patent-leather shoes; but for the most part, the whole family at leisure from Grandma down to the three-year-old will be dressed exactly the same, perpetually ready to play on the swings.

Women have seized permission to dress as male pirates and pashas or Restoration cavaliers and Romantic duellists as well as modern leather-clad outlaws; but the parodic flavor tends to give them, too, the look of children wearing harmless versions of fierce trappings—always male, since those were always the best designed and the most fun. Unfierce but lower-class ethnic and historical female rig, once worn by women leading very grim lives, may form part of the repertoire—gypsy-girls and peasant-girls and farm-girls recur in women's modes, and they, too, have been favorite little girls' costumes.

But besides invoking infant games, the parodic flavor of a great deal of ordinary fashion also stresses the way forms survive and revive, with the ability to keep their power to satisfy even when most of their actual historical meaning has been consciously discounted or forgotten. We can see how fashion permits this free play of form and its many games of allusion to serve only the art of dress, never the simple aim of direct communication, just as the language in poems serves the art of poetry.

V. NOWADAYS

INFORMALITIES

A MALE FUGITIVE from suits who wears jeans and a tee-shirt is nevertheless still clad in perfectly conventional garments partly consisting of conventional underwear; he is making use of another old tradition of sartorial revolution that brings the unseen to the surface. For women this is now being done with bras and girdles, having been done much earlier with petticoats, peignoirs, camisoles, undershirts and slips. Those have all counted as more scenes in the enterprising feminine drama of exposure; but male underwear is somewhat different. Tee-shirts began as male undershirts; but so in fact did all shirts in the dim past. The shirtsleeves costume for men still retains a socially forbidden quality in some contexts, held over from the shirt's ancient days as underwear. But tee-shirts have a stronger one, since they were originally meant to be worn *under* tailored shirts, an even more intimate protective layer.

Men's fashion has never used provocative exposure as part of a formal scheme; and shirts, once invisible under medieval doublets, became elegant status symbols when they began to emerge, not erotic elements. The important parts that showed, the collar, cuffs and some of the bosom, were incorporated into the imposing and skin-concealing surface composition, but the rest remained hidden—still underwear, still humiliating as public costume. Traditionally, a man in nothing but underwear is undignified and ridiculous, or vulnerable and perhaps even sacrificial, but symbolically stripped naked, not enticingly semi-nude.

Nevertheless, half undressed with his pants on and his coat off, he's an attractive image of unselfconscious readiness for work or play, stripped for action to his second skin, which is there to soak up the honorable sweat of his sport or labor. With the shirt collar open and the sleeves rolled up, he may indeed be very erotically exposed; but that effect, unlike deliberate feminine décolletage, only succeeds by looking artless. A man can thus be attractively undressed in ordinary shirtsleeves and trousers; but he can obviously look even more so in a tee-shirt, the under-undergarment. An extreme naked vulnerability is still there, lurking behind the zeal. The combination is very appealing.

It's therefore not surprising that tee-shirts were the other phenomenon besides jeans that swept the world in the last third of this century, encompassing all sexes and classes and nations in a universal common nakedness. On top of this artless skin now goes a favored emblem, lexical or not, something that dresses the person in a provisional tattoo, transcending mere clothing. Tee-shirts began skin-tight; but it's clear that they really make the wearer even more naked if they're loose and keep all specific bumps and hollows from intruding on the eye. Such freedom from fit only adds to the idea that the wearer is really not dressed at all; just an ambling bare body, casually flashing the message on its chest.

Because poor adolescents in cities also wore the original jeans-and-tee-shirt costume, it had the repeatedly modish look of youthful lawlessness along with its older flavor of honest work. In the 1960's, it became the new *sans-culotte* costume, the scary dress of the restive urban masses. Like the original one, it came to stay and develop great variety in all social groups. Tee-shirts and jeans keep their fashionable subversive authority, their ability to weigh heavily among any proposed set of modes and to keep looking new, chiefly because their form is old and familiar, but also because they always suggest the naked man. When women wear them they still suggest Naked Man, the universal human being, dressed in neutral bareness to show that sex is not the issue for the moment.

We live in violent times, and the violent tenor of life is clearly present in everyone's sartorial consciousness. Ordinary clothing has lately tended to suppress the enlightened modern look based on the assumption of physical safety, in favor of connoting readiness to meet physical challenges or danger—as I remarked before, armor-like clothing is once again attractive. Some version of rough gear seems to suit the atmosphere, even in the most peaceable of circumstances. Again, for one portion of the public all the graceful formalities of modern Neo-classic costume, the characteristics of neat suits and smooth dresses, have lately become associated with the rules of professional public appearance and therefore with constraint; and that brings further associations with boredom and unrisky corporeal decorum—with what used to be admired as civilized grown-up behavior, now being seen from the point of view of rebellious adolescence. The old enlightened flavors of equal but distinct male and female sexual responsibility remain attached to the clothes, but such connotations have lost credibility for leisure wear.

In a general social atmosphere inflexibly ruled "informal," social safety usually means rejecting traditionally safe clothing. Dressing up is more risky than dressing down, too much respect for the occasion is considered worse than too little. Things have shifted so that for many people, elegant clothing is worn for work, and laboring dress is worn for leisure—unless it's the wild and gaudy trappings suggesting danger of a different kind, the "dressed to kill" effect. But the actual existence of classic tailored clothes does not seem to be threatened by limiting rhetoric, only some of the original meaning and some of the earlier uses. Self-portraits of modern painters such as Matisse, for example, used to show the artist at his easel clad in a suit and tie, to show the artist as an ordinary man, just like everyone else. Lately artists paint themselves in sport or laboring costume, to show the artist at play as a worker, just like everyone else; or perhaps at work as a player; or indeed as a perpetual child.

Now that the flavor either of threat or of expected bodily risk is desirable for clothing, a serious modern elegance has come to attach itself to biker's jackets, windbreakers, pea-coats, sweatshirts, work-shirts, basketball shorts, sailor's pants, overalls, boilersuits, and all the matching shoes and hats—to the whole vocabulary of form in male dress designed for physical effort and protection, now worn for leisure by both sexes. Fine wool in muted colors, supple leather in refined textures, even silk, velvet and linen can now be used for such garments, right along with the many versions in tough cotton and synthetics. Modern esthetic care for cut, color and integrated adornment can give them a classic modern beauty, right alongside the many crude and unbeautiful versions of the same thing. The latter are, of course, also being worn by many people for their original uses.

Despite their sources in clothing meant as protection, it is ease, comfort, and freedom that are the valued qualities of tough sporting and laboring garments, especially by those for whom suits are work-clothes. They are pointedly considered off-duty costume, in direct contrast to their origins. Middle-class men and women so far do not wear them to the office or to weddings or in court, where the adult versions of elegance prevail and women keep their separate scheme. Even for casual leisure moments, however, female expression, conservative as always, can still take on its ancient forms of display—glitter, exposure, constriction, adornment—so that a man in corduroy trousers and a leather jacket may be accompanied either by a sequinned, décolleté woman with a mountain of spectacular hair, or by a woman plainly clad in similar trousers and leather jacket. In some milieux, both trouser-clad and sequinned companion might also, of course, be men.

If the path of fashion follows its usual course, predictions for the very distant future might well include a further elevation of bomber jackets and work-trousers into conventional formal dress for both sexes alike, to produce a new standard adult costume in the practical androgynous mode that has been unnoticeably evolving from innocent infant wear. A woman in a tuxedo still looks provocative, and not conventionally formal; but a woman in a zipper jacket and pants already looks purely elegant in the best tradition of classic modernity, if the garments are obeying those esthetic rules. In the fullness of time, the Senate floor may eventually have the same look we now see at the museum or the coffee-shop or the ballgame, only smoothed out, toned down and clarified. Just as in the case of the lounge-suit, such a move would still not be an innovation in form, since the basic designs for those work-jackets and work-trousers, just as for jeans and tee-shirts, have already been around for more than a century.

What would be new would be if *both sexes* normally wore them for formal professional life. The garments, of course, are all wholly masculine; if all men and women wear them for the courtroom and the boardroom and the conference table, it would mean that traditionally

OPPOSITE: Helmut Newton, fashion photograph, suit by Yves Saint Laurent, from *Vogue,* September 1975. ABOVE: Lara Rossignol, fashion photograph, suit by Rhonda Harness, from *Vogue,* November 1986.

Sexual ambiguity and erotic risk have become dominant themes in fashion photography, in an increasingly violent epoch. The two women on the menacing nocturnal street offer opposing forms of sexual display, one using nudity with a hat and high heels, the other a sharply articulated suit that suggests male nudity underneath. The couple seem well matched; but the photograph indicates that the suit is the sexier choice. The embracing man and woman have a more ambiguous relation—he is naked like a clinging baby, she is dressed to dominate and escape; or else he is Tarzan in the jungle, and she is dressed to be attacked and carried off by superior force.

feminine effects would have to be deployed entirely during leisure moments. And then, men and women would doubtless share equally in all the possibilities of skirts, gowns, veils, robes, harem pants, cosmetics, sequins, feathers, high heels, sculpted hair, varieties of décolletage and all the rest of it, borrowing freely from the increasingly available styles of other cultures and from the endless resources of history. At a party, things might start looking the way fantasy suggests they once did during the Byzantine Empire or at the court of Ashurbanipal—except that all the waiters and waitresses would be wearing modern three-piece suits.

But meanwhile, things move along slowly as usual. We have seen that a custom exists for wearing jeans and other forms of mass-produced work-trouser with conventionally tailored jackets. The mode, beginning with Ivy League students in the fifties, was in fact a return to the early look of the modern male scheme, in its use of several fabrics for one suit, with the most plebeian for the trousers. A "sport-jacket" worn with non-matching tailored slacks is an older variant, felt by conventional modern men to be an absolutely informal costume, insultingly casual for certain occasions and totally different from a "suit," even though the design, cut and fit are identical with that of one-fabric suits, and it neither provides nor suggests more physical ease. It is in fact a suit, informal only by convention—one that goes back to the revolutionary beginning of suits. Another important variant is the blazer with flannels, which has more formality because of its originally upper-class naval and yachting connotations, and is even more directly linked to the Neo-classic scheme.

We can see how the present formal suit, once known and thought of as the casual lounge-suit, with its flavor of ease and accessibility, has replaced the frock coat of old as the symbol of confining rectitude. The jacket-and-slacks costume consequently took over the look of symbolic social laxity the lounge-suit once had; and that's unsurprising, given the subversive freight an unmatched costume has always carried, hidden under the surface of its smoothly formalized versions. Breaking up the elements of the suit with either jeans or slacks is more modern in the original way. We'll see if standard elegant suits slowly fossilize under continual social pressure, and are initially replaced by jackets and trousers of different fabrics for dress wear, in yet another revolutionary step into the past.

SEXUALITIES

IT'S CLEAR that modernizing clothes for women has meant copying men's clothes, directly or indirectly, one way or another. To even the balance, however, we can see that many men in the last third of this century have already taken up the formerly female game of finding pleasure in expressive multiple guises. In one man's closet, the new, colorful leisure versions of active gear make sharp contrasts with well-cut business suits and formal sportswear like tweed jackets, classic shirts lie next to extreme sweatshirts, and everything is meant for wear in the same urban milieu. We may now find the curious spectacle of a man privately at ease fifteen stories above the city street, sipping wine and reading Trollope in a warm room furnished with fragile antiques and Persian rugs, dressed in a costume suitable for roping cattle on the plains or sawing up lumber in the North woods. Once, only women and children offered such visual effects.

Apart from such curiosities, however, the new male freedom has produced a pleasing richness of variety similar to the modern female one, though not entirely the same and still not quite so broad. But handbags, necklaces and earrings have lost their taboo for men, just as all parts of male dress have long since lost their outrageousness for women; they are licensed dress-ups when they aren't practical or elegant. Both sexes play changing games today, because for the first time in centuries men are learning clothing habits from women, instead of the other way around.

Some of what men are taking up, it must be noted, is simply male trappings that have long since gone out of use *except* by women. Purses and earrings, long hair and brilliant scarves, fanciful hats and shoes may be safely regenerated as male habits, since they have been in storage below the surface as very old and vigorous masculine traditions in the West. It does seem unlikely, however, that ancient Western female effects—voluminous skirts, creative décolletage for chest, back, and arms, bonnets or veils for the head—are likely to be taken up very soon by ordinary Western men. Men have relearned from women mainly how to be mutable and multiple, decorative and colorful, and to rediscover their hair; but the most ancient female symbolic material still remains largely taboo.

The female move to male gear, on the other hand, which was always a partial affair in the past and a firm part of the feminine erotic tradition, has lately been fully completed, and society has thoroughly internalized it. Trousers and tailoring and short hair are now wholly female in themselves, and women wearing them no longer look masculine. Women can moreover no longer imitate men specifically to be taken seriously, because male clothes are already female, too. But it follows that current male clothes have less of a uniquely masculine meaning even when men wear them, and therefore they may safely take on new flavors formerly called feminine. It's clear that during the second half of this century, women finally took over the total male scheme of dress, modified it to suit themselves, and have handed it back to men charged with immense new possibilities.

Even conventional men who don't wear long hair or earrings do wear brilliant shirts, sweaters, socks, hats and scarves in arresting shapes and colors recently seen only on women. Many modish tailored trousers, jackets and waistcoats for men are abandoning their careful dependence on tradition and branching out into the expressive exaggerations devised for women's use of them. There has recently been a mode for trousers that begin to expose the underpants and appear to fall off the hips, in an unprecedented allusion to the female vocabulary of décolletage. Male street fashion from many sources has at last had an effect on middle-class males, as it once had only on women. The general idea of fantasy and pleasure seems to have re-entered male dress through female influence— that is, through a new acknowledgment and recognition of female reality that has permitted that influence to function.

The qualities of mutability in surface design that were associated with female habits of dress for two centuries no longer need to represent weakness and madness along with attractiveness, and men no longer have to fear them. There are new eyes for the gaudy old devices that once clothed male power before the modern era, in part because bright hues, vivid hair, glitter, and skin-tight fit are attributes of the great current heroes of sport and entertainment who command vast fees and global attention. The look of male sexual potency in the post-modern world is able to float free of those austere visions of masculinity, solidified in the nineteenth century, that discredited any richness of fantasy in dress by calling it feminine.

Hair has taken on enormous expressive possibilities for men, now that everyone has acknowledged its ancient male authority, and women have naturally given up none of their modern license to play with it in public. Hair has provoked stronger feeling than anything else in the history of clothing, since it's always part of both clothes and body, both intimate and highly visible if the head is left bare. Hair's visual qualities can obviously cause keen anguish and pleasure, both to owners and observers, and it is easy to understand why some traditions have insisted that women keep theirs out of sight. Hair will do for any sort of rebellious expression; cutting it can be aggressive or renunciatory, and so can growing it. Ideas and rules about hair for men and women make constant news, and the visual effects it creates may rely on immediate responses. For men, facial hair has always shared in the general excitement about hair, and there has been constant male play with beards, sideburns and mustaches; but it should be noted that while women have been carefully painting their faces in this century, most men have been just as carefully maintaining the artificial cosmetic ritual of shaving. Both serve the essentially *pictorial* ideal of the fully dressed body, which must include the face in the composition.

In our present period of exchange, hair may be worn very short by women or very long by men without either looking transsexual, only extreme. Men not only wear long hair, they tie it back with the decorative clips and ribbon-decked elastics formerly used only by women—but it's noticeable that they usually don't wear Alice in Wonderland hairbands, which derive from hoods and veils and so far remain distinctly feminine. Headbands around the brow, by contrast, are unisex. Both sexes shave their heads, dye their hair purple or wear dreadlocks; anyone, in the androgynous infant spirit, may safely imitate the hairdressing associated with otherworldly fantasy, or seize on any headgear from other cultures. One new mode shown on strong and virtuous men in recent films is a classic tailored suit and tie, worn with a ponytail or the long curly hair once the property of girls. Even among the new male freedoms, the suit still goes down well—perhaps because it, too, has become the property of girls.

The intense power of deliberately androgynous looks has lately asserted itself publicly among adored popular performers, visually confirming the ancient idea that pleasure in sexuality may be richer if the two sexes are allowed to acknowledge their erotic affinities and are not kept stringently divided. The world has moreover finally learned that gay men and women are just as various in personal styles of dress as all other free citizens are; and so straight men and women may make new fashions out of old signals once narrowly perceived as homosexual, modes that are now attached to such former associations only by sympathy and irony, as the modern habit of fashion has taught us to use them.

REVELATIONS

THE FAMOUS "REVEALING" quality of fashion is much discussed in contemporary life. The feeling people have that their clothes are giving their secrets away comes from the knowledge that making choices among the significant visual alternatives in modern dress is not wholly under conscious control. In modern America especially, where boundaries between social groups have mattered all the more for being in constant flux, uneasiness about what clothes can express has always been acute. Our besetting itch to improve ourselves, to keep transcending unsatisfactory circumstances, beginnings and rebeginnings of all sorts, has led to a search for rules; and it has also led to a kind of fashion in America that can lead toward extreme conformity, apparently arising out of sheer anxiety. Solid belief has come to prevail in the power of external signs to mask an uncertain self, as if in a fearful retreat to the primitive conditions associated with isolated tribes.

Manufacturing and marketing clearly serve the dread of individual exposure. Makers' and designers' characteristic signals appear prominently on garments and appurtenances, and complete schemes of modish dress, denoting conscious adherence to specific modish tastes or ideas, may be adopted down to small details. In this way individual secrets can seem safe from revelation, especially individual failure of nerve and lack of esthetic self-confidence. Everyone hates to look like a fool; but especially to look like the only fool, an idiot living in a private world, hopelessly out of things, as many people may feel they really are. The feeling seems strongest among the very young, for whom looking right—that is, like everyone else—is the fiercest sartorial impulse. In high school, visibly giving in to private imaginative fantasy is socially dangerous; so platoons of students will passionately look interchangeable down to the hairclips and belt-buckles, vying only for the edge, the tiny variation that adds individual chic to the prevailing sameness; and that, too, must be the right one.

Adults continue to fear looking like fools long after high school has dispersed. For them, fashion now offers the chance to look dressed in a given genre, and visibly share in some generally desirable well-known folly—to join an available tribe. The need for personal acceptance is met by an array of acceptable impersonal guises: if you adopt one thoroughly, no one will see through it to the actual you. You will have gone into uniform or taken the veil; the honorable mantle of your chosen group will shelter you from ridicule.

It's in fact clear that "uniforms," so vigorously despised in much current rhetoric about clothes, are really what most people prefer to wear, garments in which they feel safely similar to their fellows. Once in uniform, they can choose their personal details, feel unique, and then sneer at the members of other tribes who all seem ridiculously alike in their tribal gear. For the past two centuries, men have dreaded looking like fools much more than women have; and so the dress of the male tribe has had a somewhat stronger uniform quality than the female one. Women have envied that very thing about it—and sneered at it, too.

One known reason for fashion's deep appeal is the way it provides the ability to look like everyone else, in the ancient tribal way; but at the same time, it provides a choice of tribes. Beyond that, fashion delightfully invites risky indulgence in private fantasy with a host of variations

Publicity photograph, Marlon Brando in *A Streetcar Named Desire,* 1951.

Subversive masculine modes in the second half of this century began with the tee-shirts and bluejeans of rural laborers, later adopted by rebellious urban youth. Brando shows an awareness that a tee-shirt is male underwear, and that its display is as sexy as his expression or his muscles.

and details, offered in a context of complete and perhaps confusing and deceptive freedom of choice. Seen in one way, fashion makes many look remarkably alike; seen in another way, fashion permits each to look excitingly unique. Guilt and fear about this uneasy combination never seem to lessen; it is a responsibility.

If you do find and choose what strikes your most private fancy, you will, of course reveal yourself. What will show, even if nobody is watching or interpreting the data, is which colors and shapes and styles of ornament you obsessively choose, which other ones you always avoid, which kinds of things you endlessly seek versions of—in sum, all that you might wish to hide, the things that contribute, even without your conscious desire, to the image you unconsciously long to resemble or believe you have. If you are aware that you always wear high necks, or never wear anything green, or love loose things or tight things, you will probably have plausible-sounding reasons to offer if anyone asks why. If you are a man who hates neckties, or who loves neckties, or who loves colored shirts and avoids white ones, or won't wear a hat under any circumstances, you can probably think up a reason for each. But we know fashion isn't founded on reason; the desire to summon explanations only shows that we know how irrational it makes us all seem.

Modern fashion helpfully preserves uniformity, which gives the requisite background in the preferred temporary style, while allowing the unreasoning gestures of desire and revulsion—the revelation of ineradicable unconscious wish, of ancient buried memory, of deep habits of mind—to have free play on the surface. I have remarked that the very forms clothes take ensure this, because they have evolved out of the deep fantasies common to all in a common culture. With the new freedom of personal choice unfettered by strict social codes, the individual psyche can privately illustrate itself in some detail for its own satisfaction, using the modern visual vocabulary of dress that has been accumulating for generations. The fashion business keeps feeding new surface material into the medley, permitting quick shifts of expressive theme: designers draw on their own unconscious wishes and conscious memories, hoping to find echoes in large sections of the public that keep forming new markets.

The many possible conventional shapes taken by collars and cuffs, the kinds of ornament normally applied on different parts of clothes—

straps across the raincoat shoulder, tucks down the front of a shirt, a flower on a lapel—the customary loose or tight fit of clothing for certain portions of the body, the usual placement of seams, pockets, buckles, zippers, and buttons, to say nothing of colors and color combinations, patterns and combinations of patterns, and particular fabrics for certain garments, the use of ornament formed out of abstract shapes, or out of animals and foliage—all these have gradually developed, forming an essentially variable but nevertheless fairly coherent modern sartorial image with an autonomous history. This is the foundation of modern dress, the accumulated vocabulary of modern sartorial form, filled with overlapping multiple meanings that we all inherit despite social change and even despite fashionable change. Most fashionable change will simply vary the recipe—make things out of uncustomary fabrics, put the buttons lower, make loose things tight and vice versa, or put some things out of circulation for a time, all without abandoning the ingredients, which still find deep responses in us all.

Elements have been added over time, most of which have cleverly created a new view of older conventions rather than driving them out—panty-hose, for example, which came to improve on gartered stockings without causing those to vanish but only to shift their ground. Zippers, theoretically utilitarian, have been ornamentally and suggestively used right from their beginnings in the 1920's, to keep their references vital and novel and ensure their continuing life. Very little vanishes quickly; it takes half a century or more. Styles and their psychological freight tend to linger, generating comfort and obscure satisfaction, mixing with new things that excite and seduce. The freest personal choices made among the thousands of current options may thus betray unconscious bondage to old family taboo, to ethnic or regional custom, to childhood obsession, and above all to sexual dispositions of the most basic kind, even while the surface choices follow new modish trends.

The most important further fact is, however, that much of this betrayal and bondage is unnoticeable. Choices may be governed by these inner drives, but the casual viewer sees only the general characteristics of the mode you have adopted, and judges what you want to be in broad terms without understanding why blue repels you, or why you love things tight in the waist, or why you automatically choose ornaments in silvery metal and not in gold or colors. Many strange-looking people obviously dress according to deep convictions that are not shared by on-lookers—they clearly do not know how they actually look, but are satis-fied with what their clothes make them feel and believe about their looks. These people may be the true originals, even though they are cer-tainly not the best appreciated. The famous messages of dress, the well-known language of clothes, is very often not doing any communicating at all; a good deal of it is a form of private muttering.

ANXIETIES

WITH ALL THE contradictory pressure at work in fashion, it's clear that those who are the best dressed are those with the greatest degree of self-knowledge, whatever the fashion genre—chic, anti-chic, safe, ideo-logical, urban, provincial, quirky, traditional, local, political, "Fashion-able." Such self-knowledge may indeed be purely bodily, an excellent detached understanding of one's own physical manner and appearance, instead of a treasured set of false personal myths that inhibit true vision. People may lack other kinds of self-awareness, and be cranks or bores; but with a sure inward eye for their own true physical looks, men or women may be a pleasure to look at, just for the way they choose and wear their clothes. They will never look like fools, even if the fashion they are adopting is fairly silly in itself. Sexual self-awareness underlies such physical certainty, an intuition about what enhances one's own body in motion and action in a social milieu—and what does not. You must know how your own clothed figure really behaves and appears, not how it looks in the mirror from the front, while you stand still and pose for its effect on yourself.

When it does occur, this brand of self-knowledge is usually not con-scious and therefore arguably not knowledge at all, and its effects are only another kind of unconscious revelation. To seek it consciously means to devote time and effort to specifically visual self-understanding, not to physical or moral improvement. It means deep detached study in multiple mirrors, the sort of private workout that yields real knowledge of your actual appearance: your rear views and side views, both sitting and walking, your normal head movements, your gestures and facial habits while speaking—all requiring a detailed self-regard that has itself gone out of fashion, again especially in puritan America. It is the sort of thing associated with expensive French courtesans or English Regency dandies whose only assets were their distinctive physical charms, which required constant technical maintenance backed up by ferociously clinical self-scrutiny. Spontaneity had no part in the program, and unguardedly expressing real feeling or revealing the conflicts in the individual soul were no part of the desired effect.

Modern Americans want to look sincere and spontaneous; but at the same time they don't really like to give themselves away, in case their private weaknesses seem laughable to others. Looking carefully in the mirror, so as actually to gain some understanding and possible control of the physical qualities that might give one away, smacks of caring too much, the worse weakness of all. It is much safer to rely on signs and forget real looks; to project the desire that you and your clothes be read and not really seen. The only modern citizens who are permitted and presumed to care infinitely about their real looks at every moment are performers, especially screen performers (and that includes politicians and newscasters), who have the advantage of watching miles of their own behavior on film, and who may fine-tune all physical appearance to look spontaneous for the camera while looking perfect at the same time.

Ordinary people will apparently do a great deal to avoid seeing what they actually look like, claiming not to be able to stand it, prizing good looks but disprizing themselves for caring about them, desiring to look wonderful and yet avoiding the means of doing so, feeling drawn to mirrors but loudly despising them. Instead, they will lose weight and do their working out at the gym, both of which may be good for the health and have high moral connotations, to say nothing of great social acceptance, but neither of which has any effect whatsoever on the style of movement and gesture, the customary walk, the customary facial expression, or on the way clothes are worn—that is, on real looks. And the same people will often choose clothes with strong well-known signals that stand in the way of detailed visual understanding.

The prose of fashion advertising tries to soothe the prevailing dread of unconscious self-revelation. It flatters readers by suggesting that each is really a natural aristocrat, endowed with a rich inner life that can gracefully bear exposure through personal choice in clothes, someone possessing strong instincts managed with strong self-confidence, whose whims are all creative leaps—someone whom fashion may merely serve. The productions touted are offered as tools for masterly displays of self-presentation, exemplified by the pictured models. In reality no one is fooled by any of this, and fears of not measuring up are intensified; and the suggestion lurking behind the flavor of such fashion copy is that the ideal fashion consumer has the characteristics once described as those appropriate to an artist.

An artist, according to modern and Romantic views, is in the business of unconsciously revealing his inner life only by consciously employing his skill and talent to create something external to himself, through the elements of an artistic medium. When art is working correctly, the unconscious inward dispositions of the artist support and nourish the talent he deliberately uses, and the eventual result finds a combined response in the viewer—a conscious acknowledgement of the conscious achievement, and an unconscious echo of the psychic chords the artist is unconsciously striking in himself. A good original work by an artist need not be something that breaks with the conventions of its time; it only needs to show a right harmony between the artist's idea, skill, and feeling—the evidence of an artistic self-knowledge, a personal creative story truthfully related.

Ideally, a person successfully dressed in modern fashionable clothes in any style is also just such a result, a sort of harmonious work of art made up of obscure inner impulses and clear outward choices bound together in a recognizable medium. As in all the other arts, those with more talent will produce better examples; and therein lies one of the problems with fashion. Many people feel like insufficiently talented artists, in the face of the many choices and meta-choices fashion offers.

Our great sartorial freedom and range, still especially for women, reflects the social freedom of the last quarter of a century, when social custom no longer offers strong guidance for appropriate dress. In the 1930's, it was still right or wrong to wear certain garments for certain occasions, and people knew roughly what kind of thing they needed for their normal lives; personal taste and expression had comfortable limits within which to operate. So did fashion. Persons without much imagination could at least confidently rely on dressing suitably. Lately the idea of an objective standard has been given up, except for conservative business clothes; and we know there is grumbling about that.

In all other aspects of modern living, the only standard for choice in dress is personal. You may compete or not with the prevailing choices on any occasion among any given group, so that you can go to an elegant dinner-party in a silk dress, or you can be the only one in gray flannel trousers and a sweater, or black leather and steel nail-heads; but you will in any case be judged only as someone who made that particular choice, and not as someone rightly or wrongly dressed.

We have largely reconceived dress as personal and not social theater, partly out of the modishness of the anti-fashion posture. Outward pressure to conformity is now perceived as an infringement of personal liberty. Reflecting this attitude, all personal choice is honored in formerly restrictive public circumstances. Restaurants no longer have dress codes; public black-tie events are often attended by a good proportion of men wearing informal modes. Evening dress is not prescribed at the opera; female hats are not prescribed in church. Currently accepted attitudes discourage the idea of a harmonious public picture, suggesting instead that each of us should make a satisfactory single image of our individual figure, without consideration for what the larger group will do.

Nevertheless conformity keeps on being desperately necessary to our social comfort, especially to help keep our balance in a fragmented society. The multiform fashion business obligingly provides a host of different ways to look when going to the restaurant and the opera, and we are forced to plot our course by dead reckoning. The personal burden has therefore hugely increased. We are not required to respect the occasion itself in prescribed ways; we must make up our own version of what the occasion requires of us *personally*—which everyone can then observe and judge. We are in fact forced to reveal ourselves, just like any modern artist who works out of his own drive, and not on commission for the king or the church or their equivalents.

The burden has increased because we still do not want to look like a fool. We know that our choices now make a picture story, a personal illustration of our inmost sense of our relation to the world, and that means our conformity to one group and not others. A chosen form of fashion now serves as a sort of chosen medium, a conventional form in which to cast our thoughts as well as a welcome screen to hide behind, much as social strictures used to do, and as real tribal dress is believed to do. Following a certain fashion, especially a bizarre one, can create strength in numbers all by itself, the way military dress does, masking individual fear in the guise of a general bravery. We can see it among our black urban youth, whose shared ways to dress with brilliant or outrageous verve can create success and pleasure in a grudging world.

Since there are so many fashions and kinds of fashion, we are revealed not just by our small particular choices but by our general ones, the larger strokes in which we paint ourselves, that suggest parts of the society with which we desire to be aligned, either deliberately or without realizing it. The very fashions we take up, which only emphasize those we reject, again reveal our hopeless wishes along with our high or low degree of self-knowledge; and as always in art, absolute control of the entire process is neither possible nor desirable, since the forms of modern fashion, like those of modern art, are there specifically to set free the unconscious.

Strong reaction against this state of things has held a constant counterpoint to fashion since it started. Objection to the failure of fashion to generate peace, equality, stability and beauty, to its promotion of visual disturbance, peculiarity and outrage, has spurred its development by entering into competition with it. The result has been the recurrent fashion of anti-fashion, which has speeded up the general rate of change whenever it has been most assertive. Political upheaval has sometimes been the cause of anti-fashion movements, but not usually the reason for the specific formal changes they have advocated. Those formal shifts are, as always, dictated from inside fashion itself and are then justified afterwards by reason or passion, depending on the historical moment. Anti-fashion, when it expressed itself in the form of clothing, has often simply been the next fashion, arriving a little sooner than it might otherwise have done. In this day of multiple fashions, it is just another one. Women in non-feminine trappings do not look politically opposed to their ornamented sisters so much as just fashionable in a different style.

Anti-fashion writing, preaching and legislation have had very little effect, although they have been the constant companions of fashion's life. Fashion has mainly provoked ridicule, but plenty of rage and disapproval have been aroused by its generally disrespectful quality. Since a fashion embodies a complicated secret wish, it always looks presumptuous in some way when it first appears; but the fashion-attuned contemporary world now adjusts quickly to presumption, which has acquired respectability. Fashion, while being fully as ridiculous as ever, has lately inspired much less ridicule in print than it did a generation ago. The pleasure it gives has become legitimate, along with sexual pleasure and other emotional joys. And as in the case of sex and other things, the personal problems it poses have only added to its value.

PERCEPTIONS

PERCEIVING FASHION is really done in two ways. The first is on the surface, and consists of the subjective responses we have to what's out there right now, what's in the media, what we wear and what our immediate circle wears, what people on the street have on. To respond this way, we tend to read the signs in current usage, lend ourselves to the immediate common agreements, and react as we must—we like it, we dislike it, it looks suburban, it looks ethnic, we despise it, we adore it, it looks nostalgic, it looks corporate, we reject it, we want it, we deliberately ignore it. We say, I'll never wear that, I wish I could afford one of those, that would look great on me, that's impossible for me, he shouldn't wear that, she looks great in those. Taking fashion thus directly, we have to consider only the current meaning to know how to respond appropriately; and in order to read the signs we often have to be temporarily blind to the form.

But we really are not blind. We do perceive the form, and it affects us in itself, speaking directly to our unconscious memory and fantasy just the way colors do, drawing us or repelling us as the forms in art do, whatever the style and subject; or perhaps leaving us cold the way art also may. This underlying level of appeal accounts for the lasting power of many styles and modes in modern dress which fashion seems only to manipulate but not to extinguish, changing their use and meaning but not seriously threatening their existence. On the other hand, the exciting surface phenomena in fashion that lack a steadily compelling character will easily come in and go out, be forgotten and constantly rediscovered in small fitful revivals, such as wearing a choker of black ribbon around the neck, or gloves with gauntlet cuffs. Still others may deeply repel and be adopted for a while to do just that, such as wearing garments deliberately slit into rags. These effects, too, vanish and are rediscovered.

The real changes in the inner world of collective feeling are slow, and only slow changes occur in the deep appeal of visual form in dress. Our present responses can still be called modern: only an immense cultural shift could bring about the total disappearance of trousers and jackets, for example, or of shoelaces and shirt collars, like the large change that finally did away with doublet and hose. The equally large change that finally put public trousers on women is another condition of modernity that will not extinguish soon, having taken so long to complete. Unconscious fantasy has to shift permanently before certain satisfactory propositions that underlie fashion can start failing to move the depths of the collective soul. The same deep shifts are required before tentative visions can find their true source and strike home, as in the case of short skirts in this century. Meanwhile only the small changes in extant forms are what engage our attention and invoke our present personal stake in the whole matter.

I began by saying that I always wish to consider dress as art, rather than as a sign of something else, or as a social custom linked only to other social customs. Only by looking at the history of dress as a part of the history of art, and as itself an art with a history, can we account for the actual looks of clothes and consider all of what makes them so potent. Traditions of art without named artists are particularly relevant to the history of clothes—Mayan architecture, Byzantine mosaics—for observing how the life of form can be seen to have its own phrasing. As we do with works of art, we can study the genealogy of form in clothing, learn how and where it grows out of its own earlier stages, or how and where it is deliberately copied from earlier usage, and thus discover how the phenomena of dress can do a great deal of emotional and esthetic work that goes beyond immediate social and political facts.

We can further study the purely pictorial sources for much of the formal material in clothes—pirate clothing, for example, so often evoked in modern fashion, has no truth and no life except in pictures, moving or still. Dress has its own formal past; but it has often stolen from the pictorial past simply to arrange its formal components into comprehensible images. After learning something about such sources, only then can we consider the current social significance that has attached itself to the forms, sometimes arbitrarily, and hope to come to some comprehensive understanding of the power of clothes.

Fashion has been the modernizing agent for clothes, the system that has made it possible for form in clothing to keep generating its own development and refer to itself—to turn dress into a modern art. When we study the dynamic modern form that dress has acquired in the West, we soon notice that it engages mainly with the temporal phrasing of sexuality. It doesn't just define differences between male and female dressed bodies, but describes a sexual relation that has a changing temporal life. The social meaning is dependent on the sexual one, because the sexuality is what gives the form its force, its power to have social meaning at all.

Modern masculine tailoring has been one salient example of the way form has been developed by fashion. It began by taking a set of standard, unfashionable garments in extant use that distinctively denoted currently desirable kinds of masculinity, and unifying them in a modern way into a well-integrated abstract visual scheme. The formal composition had both a fundamental sexual charge and sufficient flexibility to take on changing social meaning—to appear inclusive or exclusive, snobbish or democratic, stuffy or easy, to be grim and boring or to be sleek and subtle, to stand for ruthlessness and deception, or for candor and integrity—but also to pursue an independent and dynamic formal trajectory that has yet to reach its end.

THE REAL CHANGE displayed by all the recent sexual flexibility in dress is a new stage in the whole of fashion, representing a further leap in modern consciousness. Media existence has made all ephemeral imagery more palpable and actual, and much more important; there is no longer an absolute assumption that visual reality is one thing and visual

Lois Greenfield, fashion photograph, David Parsons of the Parsons Dance Co. in a
Calvin Klein suit, from *Men's Fashions of the Times,* March 28, 1993.

The suit is in flight toward its unknown future. All the liberties taken with the
original tailored scheme have so far not succeeded in extinguishing the form, but
only in proving its dynamic and seemingly endless possibilities.

art another. The manufacture of visual truth is big business, no longer just the province of private creative struggle, nor the province of plain deception. Clothing, now fixed in its role as a popular and commercial image-making engine, has therefore become even further removed from the unselfconsciousness of traditional custom, and more firmly lodged in the deliberate traffic of detachable visions, where "traditional custom" is simply one aspect of the traffic.

Fashion has claimed its place in a new mutable optical world where no one view of anything is acknowledged to be the true one. In a sense, fashion has simply "come out," now showing that it has always been engaged in such work; and because of the change in general consciousness, fashion has become more important and considerable as a phenomenon. It no longer goes on without being taken much note of, as something conventionally superficial and unserious and therefore unimportant. Now it is understood to be very important for that very reason. Fashion confirms the deep importance of all appearance. The burden this puts on people with limited understanding about the uses of the eye keeps getting fashion into trouble; and that further confirms its importance. We live in a world of visible projections, and we are all visible projections in it. Like it or not, we all have looks, and we are responsible for them.

Another feature of fashion's new media life is the broad education everyone is getting in the variety and quality of dress worn by the whole world. We can see and judge everything, and develop an extremely sophisticated sense of dress without even having to try. We are licensed to form strong views on the clothes of public figures, whose ensembles we can scrutinize in detail; and we can see exactly what they wear in Brussels and Jerusalem, in London and beleaguered Sarajevo, in Kuwait City and starving Somalia. Whether we pay attention or not, those details are present to us in our living rooms; no clothing is foreign, though it may be strange.

In our own world, the messages of fashions are now acknowledged to be contradictory, the action of unconscious and conscious forces are known to be clearly in play at the same time. Everyone is essentially talking to himself, like a poet. Designers merely provide the vocabulary, and the audience may kindle in response, stand in awe, or fail to notice. The famous fashion designers are more than ever like producers of films and videos than they are like craftsmen—even when they are craftsmen. They follow some trends without realizing it, while deliberately developing or avoiding others, they make canny choices in following unexamined impulses. They steal from each other. They make costly mistakes. A wish to be distinctive can make their productions extremely mannered, and that elicits unpredictable responses.

But ever since fashion broke up into separate categories, the Haute Couture no longer sets the form in which all other feminine fashion is cast; and in fact men are again setting the current tone, the disposition not to be dictated to by the whims of others. Non-famous designers of every kind provide most of our clothing, using a wide range of imaginative sources to suit many markets. Consequently designers in general are no longer perceived as tyrants, but as competent practitioners, hopeful experimenters, boldly inspired adventurers, or obviously mad gamblers. They all aim to follow the profitable flow, which mostly depends on established form, but which can only yield further profit if surprises bob up in it. The stronger the common tide on which we float, the more we want to believe that we are free; but in any case we always know we are not safe.

SELECT BIBLIOGRAPHY

Adams, Robert M. *The Roman Stamp: Frame and Facade in Some Forms of Neo-classicism.* Berkeley, Calif., 1974.

Ash, Juliet, and Lee Wright, eds. *Components of Dress: Design, Manufacturing and Image-Making in the Fashion Industry.* London and New York, 1988.

Banta, Martha. *Imaging American Women: Idea and Ideals in Cultural History.* New York, 1987.

Barbey d'Aurevilly, Jules. *Dandyism* (1844). Translated by Douglas Ainslee. New York, 1988.

Barthes, Roland. *Le Système de la mode.* Paris, 1967.

Beerbohm, Max. *Dandies and Dandies* (1896). In *Works and More.* London, 1930.

Bell, Quentin. *On Human Finery.* Rev. ed. New York, 1976.

Brain, Robert. *The Decorated Body.* New York, 1979.

Byrde, Penelope. *The Male Image.* London, 1979.

Carlyle, Thomas. *Sartor Resartus* (1835). New York, 1887.

Carman, W. Y. *British Military Uniforms.* New York, 1957.

Chaumette, Xavier. *Le Costume tailleur: La culture vestimentaire en France au XIX et XX siècles.* Paris, 1992.

Cunnington, C. Willett. *Handbook of English Costume in the Nineteenth Century.* London, 1959.

——— and Phillis. *The History of Underclothes.* London, 1951.

Davenport, Millia. *The Book of Costume.* 2 vols. New York, 1948.

Davis, Fred. *Fashion, Culture and Identity.* Chicago, 1992.

Delbourg-Delphis, Marylene. *Masculin singulier: Le dandysme et son histoire.* Paris, 1985.

De Marly, Diana. *Fashion for Men, an Illustrated History.* London, 1985.

———. *The History of Haute Couture.* London, 1980.

Dijkstra, Bram. *Idols of Perversity: Fantasies of Feminine Evil in Fin-de-Siècle Culture.* New York, 1986.

Ebin, Victoria. *The Body Decorated.* London, 1979.

Epstein, Julia, and Kristina Straub, eds. *Body Guards: The Cultural Politics of Gender Ambiguity.* New York and London, 1991.

Fairservis, Walter A. *Costumes of the East.* New York, 1971.

Flugel, J. C. *The Psychology of Clothes.* London, 1930.

Focillon, Henri. *La Vie des formes.* Paris, 1943.

Fry, Roger. *Vision and Design.* London, 1924.

Glynn, Prudence. *In Fashion: Dress in the Twentieth Century.* New York, 1978.

———. *Skin to Skin: Eroticism in Dress.* London, 1982.

Hall-Duncan, Nancy. *The History of Fashion Photography.* New York, 1979.

Hiler, Hilaire. *From Nudity to Raiment.* London, 1921.

Hollander, Anne. *Seeing Through Clothes.* New York, 1978.

Honour, Hugh. *Neo-classicism.* London, 1968.

Kidwell, Claudia, and Margaret C. Christman. *Suiting Everyone: The Democratization of Clothing in America.* Washington, D.C., 1974.

Kubler, George. *The Shape of Time: Remarks on the History of Things.* New Haven, Conn., 1962.

Kunzle, David. *Fashion and Fetishism.* Lanham, Md., 1980.

Laqueur, Thomas. *Making Sex.* Cambridge, Mass., 1990.

Laver, James. *Women's Dress in the Jazz Age.* London, 1964.

———. *Modesty in Dress.* London, 1969.

Ley, Sandra. *Fashion for Everyone: The Story of Ready-to-Wear, 1870–1970.* New York, 1970.

Lipovetsky, Gilles. *L'Empire de l'éphémère: La mode et son destin dans les sociétés modernes.* Paris, 1987.

Lynam, Ruth, ed. *Paris Fashion: The Great Designers and Their Creations.* London, 1972.

Martin, Paul. *European Military Uniforms: A Short History.* London, 1963.

Martin, Richard, and Harold Koda. *Jocks and Nerds: Men's Style in the Twentieth Century.* New York, 1989.

Milbank, Caroline Reynolds. *Couture: The Great Designers.* New York, 1985.

Molloy, John T. *Dress for Success.* New York, 1975.

———. *The Woman's Dress for Success Book.* New York, 1977.

Moore, Doris Langley. *Fashion through Fashion Plates, 1771–1970.* London, 1971.

Oakes, Alma, and Margot Hamilton Hill. *Rural Costume.* London and New York, 1970.

Pellegrin, Nicole. *Les Vêtements de la liberté.* Paris, 1989.

Perrot, Philippe. *Les Dessus et les dessous de la bourgeoisie.* Paris, 1981.

———. *Le Travail des apparences.* Paris, 1984.

Pevsner, Nikolaus. *An Outline of European Architecture.* Rev. ed. London, 1975.

Polhemus, Ted, and Lynn Procter. *Fashion and Anti-fashion: An Anthropology of Clothing and Adornment.* London, 1978.

Ribeiro, Aileen. *Dress and Morality.* New York, 1986.

———. *Dress in Eighteenth-Century Europe, 1715–1789.* New York, 1985.

Rosenblum, Robert. *Transformations in Late Eighteenth-Century Art.* Princeton, N.J., 1967.

Rudofsky, Bernard. *Are Clothes Modern?* New York, 1947.

———. *The Unfashionable Human Body.* New York, 1978.

Schoeffler, O. E., and William Gale. *Esquire's Encyclopedia of 20th Century Men's Fashions.* New York, 1973.

Simmel, Georg. "Fashion." *The International Quarterly,* vol. 10, October 1904.

Snowden, James. *The Folk Dress of Europe.* New York, 1979.

Squire, Geoffrey. *Dress and Society, 1560–1970.* New York, 1974.

Steele, Valerie. *Fashion and Eroticism.* New York, 1985.

———, and Claudia Kidwell. *Men and Women, Dressing the Part.* Washington, D.C., 1989.

Walkley, Christina. *The Ghost in the Looking-Glass: The Victorian Seamstress.* London, 1981.

Warner, Marina. *Joan of Arc.* New York, 1981.

Wilson, Elizabeth. *Adorned in Dreams: Fashion and Modernity.* Berkeley, Calif., 1988.

INDEX

INDEX

KODANSHA GLOBE

International in scope, this series offers distinguished books that explore the lives, customs, and mindsets of peoples and cultures around the world.

To order, contact your local bookseller or call 1-800-788-6262 (mention code G1). For a complete listing of titles, please contact the Kodansha Editorial Department at Kodansha America, Inc., 114 Fifth Avenue, New York, NY 10011.